HEIDI

Written by Johanna Spyri

Teacher Guide

based on translation by Eileen Hall

MEMORIA PRESS
www.MemoriaPress.com

HEIDI
Written by Johanna Spyri
based on translation by Eileen Hall

TEACHER GUIDE

ISBN 978-1-61538-055-8

Cover illustration by Starr Steinbach

Contents

PREPARING TO READ:

REVIEW

- Orally review any previous vocabulary.
- Review the plot of the book as read so far.
- Periodically review the concepts of character, setting, and plot.

STUDY GUIDE PREVIEW

- Reading Notes:
  - Read aloud together
  - This section gives the students key characters, places, terms that are relevant to a particular time period, etc.
- Vocabulary:
  - Read aloud together so that students will recognize words when they come across them in their reading.
- Comprehension Questions:
  - Read through these questions with students to encourage purposeful reading.

READING:

- Student reads the chapter (or selection of the chapter for that lesson) independently or to the teacher (for younger students).
- For younger students, you can alternate between teacher-read and student-read passages. Model good reading skills. Encourage students to read expressively and smoothly. Teacher may occasionally take oral reading grades.
- While reading, mark each vocabulary word as you come across it.
- Have students take note in their study guide margin of pages where a comprehension question is answered.

AFTER READING:

VOCABULARY

- Look at each word within the context that it is used, and help your students come up with the best synonym that defines the word. (Make sure students know the meaning of the synonym.)
- Record the word's meaning in the students' study guides. (Use students' knowledge of Latin and other vocabulary to decipher meanings.)

COMPREHENSION QUESTIONS

- Older students can answer these questions independently, but younger students (2nd-4th) need to answer the questions orally, form a good sentence, and then write it down, using correct punctuation, capitalization, and spelling. (You may want to write the sentence down for younger students after forming it orally, and then let students copy it perfectly.)
- It is not necessary to write the answer to every question. Some may be better answered orally.
- Answering questions and composing answers is a valuable learning activity. Questions require students to think; writing a concise answer is a good composition exercise.

QUOTATIONS AND DISCUSSION QUESTIONS

- Use the Quotations and Discussion Questions section of each lesson as a guide to your oral discussion of the key concepts in the chapter that may not be covered in the comprehension questions.
- These talking points can take your oral discussion to a higher level than covered in the students' written work. Use this time as an opportunity to introduce higher-level thinking. You can introduce concepts the students may not be mature enough to fully understand yet but that would be beneficial for them to begin thinking about.
- A key to the Discussion Questions is in the back of the Teacher Guide.

ENRICHMENT

- The Enrichment activities include composition, copywork, dictation, research, mapping, drawing, poetry work, literary terms, and more.
- This section has a variety of activities in it, but the most valuable activity is composition. Your students should complete at least one composition assignment each week. Proof students' work and have students copy composition until grammatically perfect. Insist on clear, concise writing. For younger students, start with 2-3 sentences, and do the assignment together. The students can form good sentences orally as you write them down, and then the students copy them.
- These activities can be completed as time and interest allow. Do not feel you need to complete all of these activities. Choose the ones that you feel are the best use of your

UNIT REVIEW AND TESTS

- There is a unit review and a quiz or test following every few lessons (varies by individual guide).
- On the weeks that have these reviews and tests, you may want to do the review early in the week, and then drill it orally a couple of times before giving the test at the end of the week.
- A final comprehensive test is also included.

Reading Notes

Detie	Heidi's aunt who has taken care of her
Heidi	young, orphaned girl
Barbie	Detie's friend
Unclè Alp	Heidi's grandfather; Tobias' father
Tobias & Adelheid	Heidi's father and mother
Bridget	Peter's mother
Grannie	Peter's grandmother

Vocabulary

Write the meaning of each bold word or phrase.

1. trudging uphill on a pair of **hobnailed** boots. nailed soles
2. The old man lived up on the mountain like a **hermit**. loner; withdrawn from others
3. That made him more angry then ever, and **morose** too. gloomy

Comprehension Questions

Answer the following in complete sentences.

1. How did Detie acquire Heidi? Why does Detie take Heidi to Uncle Alp? Heidi's parents died. When Heidi became an orphan, Detie (her aunt) and Heidi's grandmother took Heidi in. After Heidi's grandmother died, Detie got a job offer with a family in Frankfurt, so she is taking Heidi to Uncle Alp.

2. How is Uncle Alp perceived by the townspeople? Why? He is odd, antisocial, and not a churchgoer. He is scary with a wild-looking, bristly, dreadful beard. He lives as a hermit and isn't to be trusted. Generally, one might disapprove of him because of his past.

3. Describe the scenery surrounding Uncle Alp's hut. The hut stands on a little plateau on high pasture with a glorious valley view. Three old fir trees are behind the hut; beyond them are the mountains. Above the hut is grazing land; tangled undergrowth leads up to rugged peaks.

Quotations

"I've looked after her up to now, but I don't mind telling you, I'm not going to turn down a good job like the one I've just been offered, because of her."

Who said this? Detie About whom? Heidi

"She can look after herself, though she's only five. She's got all her wits about her. She knows how to make the best of things too …"

Who said this? Detie About whom? Heidi

"Then one day we heard that he'd gone to live up on the mountain and wasn't coming down any more. He's actually stayed up there from that day to this, at odds with God and man, as they say."

Who said this? Detie About whom? Uncle Alp

Discussion Questions

1. What does the first quote above tell us about Detie's character? Do you agree or disagree with her analysis of the situation? Why?
2. The author tells us that Detie is "really far from easy in her mind about what she [is] doing." What are the reasons for her uneasiness?
3. What does it mean to be "at odds with God and man"? What are the reasons for Uncle Alp choosing this lifestyle?
4. With what we know about Uncle Alp and Heidi so far, how do you think Heidi and Uncle Alp are going to get along?

Enrichment

1. Locate the towns of Mayenfield and Dorfli on a map.
2. Read the story of the prodigal son from the Bible (Luke 15). How is Uncle Alp similar to the prodigal son, and how is he different? Uncle Alp and the prodigal son left their families to "ape the gentry" and travel. Both sons wasted their inheritance on worthless things. It does not appear that Uncle Alp realizes the folly of his ways. Uncle Alp also does not return to find his family eager to reconcile with him.
3. On a separate sheet of paper, draw Heidi's family tree and include the following people: Tobias, Heidi, Detie, Uncle Alp, Adelheid, Tobias' grandmother, Detie's grandmother.

Reading Notes

cupboard a closet with shelves for dishes, cups, etc.
loft a room or storage area within a sloping roof

Vocabulary

Write the meaning of each bold word or phrase.

1. a biggish room, the whole **extent** of his living quarters. scope, limit, size
2. and blew up the fire with **bellows** till it was red and glowing. air blowing device
3. Two graceful animals **detached** themselves from the others. separated
4. The moon, which had been covered by **scudding** clouds ragged and swiftly moving

Comprehension Questions

Answer the following in complete sentences.

1. Describe the inside of Grandfather's hut and cupboard. Grandfather's hut is one room with a loft. His only furniture is a table, chair, and bed. He has a stove and a pot, plus a cupboard with shelves containing clothes, cups, plates, and glasses. On top is a loaf of bread, meat, and cheese.

2. What are the names of Grandfather's goats? Why are those names appropriate? Daisy and Dusky are the goats. Daisies are flowers that are mostly white; so is Daisy. Dusky is brown in color; dusky is an adjective that means dark in color.

3. What does Grandfather do to make Heidi feel more comfortable in the hut? He provides her with a coarse cloth and heavy linen from his own bed. He feeds Heidi and makes accommodations by fixing her a table just her size. He makes her a high chair. He checks on her in the loft and stays with her for a while.

Quotations

At first Heidi just stood and watched with great interest, then she thought of something else and ran to the cupboard. When her grandfather brought the steaming pot and the toasted cheese to the table, he found it was laid with two plates, two knives, and the round loaf.

A strong wind sprang up again, whistling and rustling through the fir trees. The sound pleased Heidi so much that she began dancing and jumping about, and her grandfather stood watching her from the door of the shed.

Discussion Questions

1. In the first quote above and throughout the chapter, Heidi watches Grandfather with great interest. Find two other places in the chapter where Heidi observes Grandfather and tell why you think she does so.
2. In this chapter, Heidi proves herself to be willing to work. Give examples supporting this statement.
3. Do you think the townspeople are correct or incorrect in their thoughts about Uncle Alp (from Chapter 1)? Why? Give examples of specific actions to support your opinion.
4. There are two illustrations in this chapter. Describe what is occurring in each picture.

Enrichment

1. Heidi tells Grandfather that the goat's milk he gives her is the best she's ever drunk. Try some goat's milk and see if you agree with Heidi's estimation of it.
2. Copy or write from dictation the second to last paragraph in the chapter. ____________

   Her grandfather went to bed also before it was dark, for he always got up with the sun, and that came over the mountain tops very early in the summer. During the night the wind blew so hard that it shook the whole hut and made its beams creak. It shrieked down the chimney and brought one or two of the old fir trees' branches crashing down. So after a while the old man got up, thinking, "The child may be frightened."

IN THE FIELDS

The little cares that fretted me,
I lost them yesterday
Among the fields above the sea,
Among the winds at play;
Among the lowing of the herds,
The rustling of the trees;
Among the singing of the birds,
The humming of the bees.

The foolish fears of what might pass—
I cast them all away
Among the clover-scented grass,
Among the new-mown hay;
Among the husking of the corn,
Where drowsy poppies nod,
Where ill thoughts die and good are born,
Out in the fields with God.

—Elizabeth Barrett Browning

Poetry Link!

Use the following questions to discuss the poem.

1. What does "fretted" mean? What is responsible for causing the author to fret?
   to cause to be uneasy; little cares
2. What are lowing herds?
   sounds uttered by cattle
3. What makes the rustling sound?
   leaves in the trees
4. How many syllables are in each line? Write the number at the end of each line.
   8 or 6
5. What literary device do you notice in the poem?
   repetition (use of the word "among" to begin lines) and imagery
6. Why are "fears of what might pass" foolish?
   Why should you fear things that might not even happen?
7. How do you cast fears away?
   try not to think about them
8. What is clover?
   a grass that blooms and attracts bees; also used for hay
9. What are corn husks?
   tough leaves covering an ear of corn
10. What are drowsy poppies?
    flowers having nodding buds
11. What are ill thoughts?
    bad thoughts
12. What feeling does this poem leave you with?
    Answers will vary.

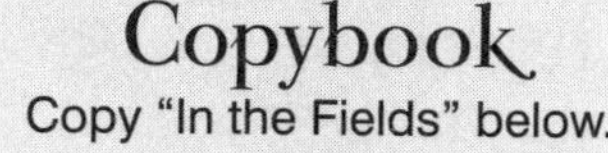

Copy "In the Fields" below.

Reading Notes

Ursula	Heidi's former caregiver
ravine	a narrow, steep-sided valley
hillock	a small hill
summit	peak; highest point
kid	baby goat

Vocabulary

Write the meaning of each bold word or phrase.

1. Peter held out the bag which contained his **meagre (meager)** lunch. poor
2. He lay down in the sun to rest after the **strenuous** climb. tough; active
3. Turk was too astonished at such **impudence** to make a fight. boldness; disrespect
4. Finch, highly **indignant** at such treatment, struggled wildly. offended; insulted

Comprehension Questions

Answer the following in complete sentences.

1. Name the special goats in Peter's herd with a distinguishing feature for each. Big Turk has strong horns and is always trying to butt the others. Finch is a frisky kid with sharp horns. Snowflake is a little white orphaned goat.

2. How does Heidi help save Finch? Heidi lures Finch from the ravine's edge with grass to eat.

3. Heidi believes she saw a fire on the mountain. Describe what she saw. How does Grandfather explain the sight? The setting sun spread a glow over everything, turning the mountains and trees different colors. Grandfather says the sun was saying good night to the mountains in a way that they would not forget him during the night.

Quotations

"You must have a wash first, or the sun will laugh to see you look so black."

Who said this? Grandfather To whom? Heidi

"They wanted to stay in the sun and didn't like being shut up in your apron."

Who said this? Grandfather About whom? the meadow flowers

"You can imagine he's saying, 'If only you would all mind your own business and climb up to the mountain tops as I do, you'd be a lot better off.'"

Who said this? Grandfather About whom? the hawk

"It's the sun's way of saying good night to the mountains. He spreads that beautiful light over them so that they won't forget him till he comes back in the morning."

Who said this? Grandfather To whom? Heidi

Discussion Questions

1. The quotes above show the creative way Grandfather explains everyday events to Heidi. Why does Grandfather explain things in this way? Think of some examples of this from your own experience and discuss.
2. What does the third quote above tell you about Uncle Alp?
3. Heidi feels a special bond with Snowflake. What are the reasons for this bond?

Enrichment

1. In this chapter, the names are given for several of the mountains. Try to locate some pictures of these specific mountains.
2. Heidi greatly enjoys her time on the mountain with Peter. Use the topic sentence given and write a paragraph with at least three supporting sentences.

Heidi had a wonderful day on the mountain full of many new experiences

Answers will vary. Possible supporting ideas would be:
picking flowers
enjoying the beautiful view
seeing the hawk
learning about the goats
sunset on the mountains

Reading Notes

spinning to make yarn by drawing out, twisting, and winding fibers
darning mending with needle and yarn
eightfold eight layers
mend to make something usable by repairing; to fix

Vocabulary

Write the meaning of each bold word or phrase.

1. He **plunged** his arms deep into a big pot of milk. pushed
2. Peter's hut seemed **wretchedly** cramped. miserably
3. Grannie did not **contradict** her. to disagree with
4. "… the place is really falling down," she cried **tremulously**. fearfully; with trembling

Comprehension Questions

Answer the following in complete sentences.

1. What does Grandfather do during the winter months? What does Peter do? Grandfather does his carpentry and makes the goat's milk cheese. Peter has to go to school to learn to read and write.

2. Peter has two nicknames in this chapter. What are they? Heidi's grandfather calls him the General (general of the herd), and Grannie calls him Peterkin.

3. According to Bridget, what does Heidi look like? She is thin like her mother, but she has black eyes and curly hair like Tobias and the old man.

4. Why does Grannie wish Peter could read? Grannie wants Peter to be able to read hymns to her from an old prayer book.

5. What two things upset Heidi about her visit with Grannie? What is Heidi's solution? She is upset that Grannie cannot see and that Grannie is afraid the house will collapse on them. Heidi believes Grandfather will be able to fix everything.

Quotations

But Heidi was happy wherever she was. Of course she loved going up the mountain where there was always so much to see, but she also enjoyed going round with her grandfather, watching him at his carpentry and all the other jobs.

That strange music in the tree tops had a special fascination for her and she could not stay indoors when she heard it.

This quote is about whom? Heidi

"Come here, my dear, and listen to me. I can't see, but I can hear, and when one is blind, it is so good to hear a friendly voice, and yours I love already."

Who said this? Grannie To whom? Heidi

"That's enough. I know quite well what you really think of me. Go indoors. I can see for myself what wants doing."

Who said this? Uncle Alp To whom? Bridget

Discussion Questions

1. What clues does the author give that Peter's Grannie is blind?
2. What is your opinion of Uncle Alp's response to Bridget (4th quote above)?
3. Contrast Grannie's outlook on life before and after Heidi starts to visit. How does the third quote above relate to your answer?

Enrichment

1. Copy, or write from dictation, the last paragraph of the chapter.

Heidi grew very fond of Peter's Grannie, and when she understood that no one could make her see again, she was very sad. But as Grannie told her over and over again that she didn't mind being blind nearly so much when Heidi was with her, she came down on the sledge with her grandfather every fine day. He always brought his hammer and nails and any other materials needed, and gradually he repaired the whole cottage, so that Grannie was no longer frightened by noises at night.

Reading Notes

bleating goat cry
threshold entrance to a house or building
Pastor Uncle Alp's former neighbor from Dorfli
paralyz(s)ed affected by a loss of voluntary movement in a body part caused by injury or disease of the nerves, brain, or spinal cord
truant a student absent from school without permission

Vocabulary

Write the meaning of each bold word or phrase.

1. Detie tossed her head in **exasperation**. great annoyance
2. Detie was all **amiability**, and started to talk at once. friendliness
3. Don't be stupid and **obstinate** like one of those old goats! stubborn
4. She called **beseechingly**, "Don't take the child away from us!" in a desperate, pleading way

Comprehension Questions

Answer the following in complete sentences.

1. What does the pastor want Grandfather to do? He wants him to send Heidi to school and move down the mountain and live in Dorfli. He also wants Grandfather to make peace with God and his neighbors.

2. Why does Detie return for Heidi? The family Detie works for has some rich relatives in Frankfurt that have a little girl living there who is paralysed and is in need of a playmate.

3. What does Detie say to Heidi to convince her to go along with her? Detie tells her that Grandfather is angry and wants her to go. She also says Frankfurt is very nice, but she can come back if she does not like it.

4. Contrast the two times that Detie comes down the mountain. The first time Detie left Heidi with Grandfather, the townspeople could not understand why she would leave Heidi with him. This time, the townspeople think she is saving her.

Quotations

"Won't you, for her sake, do what you should have done long ago—come back to Dorfli to live? What sort of a life do you lead up here, at odds with God and man?"

Who said this? the pastor To whom? Uncle Alp

From that day Uncle Alp grew more silent and forbidding than ever. On the rare occasions when he passed through Dorfli with his basket of cheeses on his back and a heavy stick in his hand, mothers kept their children well out of the way, for he looked so wild.

Discussion Questions

1. Contrast Grandfather's view of formal schooling with the pastor's.
2. Contrast Detie's view of the goats to Heidi's.
3. What is your opinion of Detie taking Heidi to Frankfurt?
4. How does Heidi's leaving affect Grandfather? Grannie?

Enrichment

1. Locate Frankfurt, Germany, on a map. Check the distance between Dorfli and Frankfurt.
2. This version of *Heidi* uses some spellings of words that will look strange to an American English reader. This is because there are a few words in the English language that have different spellings than the British spellings. The British words add a "u" in the spellings. [Example: color, colour] Directions: Write below three words in this chapter that use British spellings. After each, write the American spellings.

neighbour (p. 57)	neighbor
humour (p. 60)	humor
Frankfurt, Germany (p. 63)	Frankfort, KY

3. In this chapter, Heidi is taken away from a place she loves and people she loves. Write a paragraph telling how you think you would feel if you were in Heidi's position.

Answers will vary.

Reading Notes

Mr. Sesemann	wealthy owner of home in Frankfurt; Clara's father
Clara	Mr. Sesemann's sickly daughter
Miss Rottenmeier	housekeeper in charge of the servants and caring for Clara
John	coachman
Sebastian	manservant
Tinette	maid
Mr. Usher	Clara's tutor
christen	to give a name to at baptism

Vocabulary

Write the meaning of each bold word or phrase.

1. A maid appeared, with … a **pert** look on her face. bold; spirited
2. "Is the child **halfwitted** …" stupid
3. "… or **impertinent**?" rude
4. Then she called, in a **peremptory** tone, for Tinette. commanding

Comprehension Questions

Answer the following in complete sentences.

1. Why does Miss Rottenmeier seem unimpressed with Heidi? Heidi's apparel is shabby; she disapproves of Heidi's facial expression of astonishment and her manners, Heidi's response to her questions, Heidi's age, and Heidi's inability to read.

2. How does Detie respond to Miss Rottenmeier's negative impression of Heidi? She reassures Miss Rottenmeier that Heidi is not impertinent, but bright. She asks Miss Rottenmeier to excuse Heidi's manners and pretends Heidi is older than she is. She makes a quick exit out of the room and leaves Heidi there.

3. What is dinner like for Heidi the first night of her stay at the Sesemann house?
   1. A lesson in table manners
   2. Perplexing for Heidi (she is inexperienced in being served by a servant)
   3. Lecture in daily behavior

Quotations

"If you please, I thought she would be just what you were looking for, Ma'am. You told me you wanted an unusual sort of child, and there's nothing unusual about the older ones. They are all alike. But Heidi is different."

Who said this? Detie To whom? Miss Rottenmeier

Miss Rottenmeier came back at this point. She had not been quick enough to catch Detie, and was very much put out, for she did not see how to get out of this awkward situation, for which she was really responsible as she had certainly agreed to Heidi's being fetched.

Discussion Questions

1. What character traits does Detie exhibit in her encounter with Miss Rottenmeier?
2. What are possible solutions to Miss Rottenmeier's problem in the second quote?
3. What is the scene depicted in the chapter's illustration? Try to identify the characters using clues from the chapter to help you.

Enrichment

1. Clara mentions taking a dose of cod liver oil if she is feeling ill. Cod liver oil has long been taken for medicinal purposes and is still used as a supplement today. Research the history and current use of cod liver oil.
2. Copy, or write from dictation, the conversation about reading between Heidi and Miss Rottenmeier from page 72. Notice spelling and punctuation.

She turned to Heidi and went on, "What books have you been using in your lessons?"

"None," said Heidi.

"What's that you say? How did you learn to read then?"

"I haven't learnt to read," Heidi replied. "Nor has Peter."

"Good gracious me, can't read at your age!" cried Miss Rottenmeier in dismay. "Impossible! What have you learnt then?"

"Nothing," said Heidi frankly.

Reading Notes

hurdy-gurdy small musical organ played by turning a crank
tortoise another name for a turtle
twopence two pennies

Vocabulary

Write the meaning of each bold word or phrase.

1. He was **waylaid** by Miss Rottenmeier. stopped or intecepted by someone
2. after several politely **consoling** remarks comforting
3. She was most surprised to see what **havoc** she had wrought. great destruction or damage
4. She said, looking very **crestfallen**, "It isn't a bit what I expected." disappointed; discouraged

Comprehension Questions

Answer the following in complete sentences.

1. Why does Miss Rottenmeier delay the tutor? She wants to encourage him to help in her plot to send Heidi back home. If he will say that schooling Heidi and Clara together will hold Clara back, then maybe Mr. Sesemann will send Heidi home.
2. How does Mr. Usher try to console Miss Rottenmeier? He suggests that Heidi might be advanced in some ways and she might be able to catch up quickly.
3. What is Heidi trying to find in the city, and why? What does she find? Heidi is accustomed to going outside every day, so she is trying to find a place from which she can see nature. From the high tower, she sees only rooftops and towers, not what she hoped to see.
4. Compare Miss Rottenmeier's reaction to the kittens with Sebastian's. She is terrified of them and wants them removed. He likes them and helps to hide them.

Quotations

"I will speak to you later, Adelheid. Now I will only say that it was extremely naughty of you to leave the house without asking permission or saying a word to anyone, and then to go roaming about until this late hour. I've never heard of such a thing."

Who said this? Miss Rottenmeier

The scolding which Miss Rottenmeier had intended to give Heidi had to be put off until next day, for she felt quite worn out with all she had been through of anxiety and annoyance, anger and fright. Consequently she withdrew very soon to her room, and Clara and Heidi went happily to bed, knowing that the kittens were safe.

Discussion Questions

1. Why is Heidi compared to "a wild bird in a cage"?
2. Heidi is having a difficult start to her stay in Frankfurt. Miss Rottenmeier is very upset by Heidi's behavior, as shown in the first quote. Do you think Miss Rottenmeier is correct or incorrect in her assessment of Heidi's actions? Why?
3. From the second quote above, summarize what made Miss Rottenmeier anxious, annoyed, angry, and afraid.

Enrichment

1. The boy in this chapter carries a small hurdy-gurdy on his back. The term *hurdy-gurdy* was used for an instrument known as a barrel organ. The barrel organ has pre-set songs that play at the turn of a crank.
2. There are so many things that occur in this one day for Heidi. Make a timeline of Heidi's day, using brief descriptions of what she was doing at each time given below. Use the chapter's major events as your guide.

8:00 a.m. Heidi wakes up, tries to look out the window; Tinette calls her to breakfast
8:30 a.m. Heidi is brought to breakfast by Miss Rottenmeier
10:15 a.m. Mr. Usher arrives in the study for tutoring
10:30 a.m. Heidi hears the carriages, runs out of the room, and upsets the table
10:45 a.m. Miss Rottenmeier takes Heidi to see the mess she made
11:00-12:00 Lunch; rest time for Clara begins
12:30 p.m. Heidi asks Sebastian to open the window so she can see what is outside
12:40 p.m. Heidi runs outside to find the church tower
12:45 p.m. Heidi meets the boy with the hurdy-gurdy
12:45-6:00 p.m. Heidi is out, goes up the church tower; plays with the kittens
6:00-6:20 p.m. Miss Rottenmeier scolds Heidi; kittens appear; Miss Rottenmeier leaves
8:00 p.m. Everyone goes to bed after a full day

Reading Notes

savage an uncivilized person
dust bin a garbage can
street urchin a child who spends most of his time on the streets

Vocabulary

Write the meaning of each bold word or phrase.

1. he began **pompously** proudly; importantly
2. she **summoned** Sebastian and Tinette to the study. to call someone to appear
3. Tinette either spoke to her in the most **disdainful** way scornful; looking down upon
4. or **mimicked** her, and Heidi knew she was being made fun of. copied; imitated

Comprehension Questions

Answer the following in complete sentences.

1. What strange occurrences are the result of Heidi's escapades to the church? The boy who led Heidi to the church comes to the house, plays his organ, and collects some money. His tortoise frightens Rottenmeier. The rest of the kittens are delivered, causing another uproar.

2. How is Heidi comforted by Sebastian and Clara? Clara suggests they wait until her father returns to see what will happen. She offers fresh rolls. Sebastian offers to play with her and the kittens later.

3. Miss Rottenmeier thinks Heidi has gone quite mad. What makes her think this? Heidi becomes upset when she is not allowed to leave and tells Miss Rottenmeier all the things she is missing from home. Miss Rottenmeier doesn't understand Heidi's homesickness.

4. What is Mr. Usher's opinion of Heidi? Mr. Usher likes Heidi and thinks she is normal in many ways. He worries that she has trouble learning the alphabet.

Quotation

"I want to go home because while I'm here Snowflake will be crying, and Grannie will be missing me too. And here I can't see the sun saying good night to the mountains. And if the hawk came flying over Frankfurt he'd croak louder than ever because there are such a lot of people here being horrid and cross, instead of climbing high up where everything's so much nicer."

Discussion Questions

1. Read the quote above. Imagine you are Miss Rottenmeier and you don't know much about Heidi's life before she came to you. What about Heidi's quote above would seem strange to you?
2. What is the relationship between Heidi and Sebastian? How has it changed since the beginning of Heidi's time in Frankfurt?
3. Heidi's original plan was to go back to the mountains the day after she arrived in Frankfurt. In this chapter, she decides to stay. What are the reasons for her staying in Frankfurt?

Enrichment

1. Heidi secretly collected rolls for Grannie. Why would she hoard food? Write a paragraph explaining Heidi's reason for hiding the food. Explain why this was a good idea and why it was a bad idea. Use the first sentence of these directions as your topic sentence.

Answers will vary.

Reading Notes

regards sentiments of esteem or affection
fortnight 14 days and nights; 2 weeks

Vocabulary

Write the meaning of each bold word or phrase.

1. because of her prolonged **sojourn** in the mountains visit; temporary stay
2. for she did not particularly **relish** this news. to enjoy
3. Mr. Usher will **bear me out** about that. agree with
4. Heidi **encountered** such a forbidding look to come upon or meet with

Comprehension Questions

Answer the following in complete sentences.

1. What does Miss Rottenmeier mean by "a real child of nature"? She means a child that has lived in a way that she considers primitive—unspoiled.

2. What is Miss Rottenmeier's ideal image of a companion for Clara? She would prefer someone Clara's own age who knows how to read. She also wants someone who behaves as children in her idea of society behave.

3. Describe who Heidi meets and talks with when she goes to fetch water. She describes him as having a nice smile, gold watch chain, and a walking stick with a horse's head handle. It was the doctor.

4. What piece of news does Miss Rottenmeier receive that causes her to be disappointed? Mr. Sesemann tells her that Heidi is going to stay. He also reminds her to make sure Heidi is treated kindly.

Quotations

"I think even Swiss children must put their feet on the ground if they want to get anywhere, otherwise they'd have been given wings."

Who said this? Mr. Sesemann To whom? Miss Rottenmeier

Mr. Sesemann had not taken her earlier complaints seriously, but this was another matter and, if true, Clara might come to some harm. He looked at the woman as though wondering whether she herself was quite right in the head …

Who is Mr. Sesemann thinking about? Miss Rottenmeier

Clara was delighted, and talked so much about Grandmamma that Heidi began to speak of her as Grandmamma too. Miss Rottenmeier frowned when she heard her, but the little girl was so used to seeing disapproval on that face that she did not pay much attention to it.

Discussion Questions

1. What is the relationship between Mr. Sesemann and Clara?
2. In the second quote, what "matter" is Mr. Sesemann concerned about? Why is he concerned?
3. How did Mr. Sesemann decide that Heidi should stay in Frankfurt?
4. How was Heidi's errand to get water an example of her "funny little ways"?

Enrichment

1. Mr. Sesemann asks Mr. Usher about his opinion of Heidi, but becomes frustrated with his "roundabout fashion" of answering questions. Read Mr. Usher's response to Mr. Sesemann and summarize what he says.
2. Copy, or write from dictation the first paragraph of the chapter.

There was a great bustle in the big house and much running up and down stairs a few days later, for the master had returned from his travels, and Sebastian and Tinette had one load of luggage after another to carry up from the carriage, for Mr. Sesemann always brought a lot of presents and other nice things home with him.

Reading Notes

Grandmamma	Clara's paternal grandmother; Mrs. Sesemann
gravely	seriously, solemnly
surname	family name; last name

Vocabulary

Write the meaning of each bold word or phrase.

1. She had pretty white hair and wore a **dainty** lace cap. delicate
2. Heidi was afraid of **vexing** her if she told her the truth. irritating
3. She did not mean to be **deprived** of any of her authority. lacking or kept from something one needs
4. She might do something useful if she had the **inclination**. a liking or preference
5. She dreamed of the mountains so **vividly** with clarity and detail

Comprehension Questions

Answer the following in complete sentences.

1. How does Grandmamma undermine the authority that Miss Rottenmeier demands?
   Grandmamma contradicts Rottenmeier and defends Heidi. She also calls Heidi by the name she has always known, rather than the names Rottenmeier has given her.

2. Why is Heidi sad in this chapter? Why does she keep it a secret? Heidi has realized that she cannot go home whenever she wants to. She chooses not to tell the Sesemanns because she doesn't want to upset them or have them think that she is ungrateful.

3. Grandmamma notices Heidi's sadness. What does she suggest Heidi do? She instructs Heidi that you can always tell God about your troubles even when you can't tell anyone else. God will help us when we ask.

4. What causes the sudden change in Heidi's ability to read? Grandmamma convinces Heidi that she would be able to read if she tried. Peter's inability to read is abnormal. Grandmamma also promises to give her a book when she learns to read.

Quotations

Indeed everything about Grandmamma was delightful to Heidi. She had pretty white hair and wore a dainty lace cap, with two broad ribbons which fluttered behind, as though there was always a gentle breeze blowing round her. Heidi thought that specially attractive.

"Now listen to me, Heidi, you've never learnt to read because you believed what Peter told you. Now you must believe what I say, that in a little while you will be able to read quite well, as most children do, being on the whole like you and not like Peter."

Who said this? Grandmamma

A change had come over Heidi since the day she had tried to go home and Miss Rottenmeier had given her such a scolding. She now understood that, in spite of what Detie had told her, she could not go away when she wanted to, and that she would have to stay in Frankfurt for a long time, perhaps for ever.

Discussion Questions

1. Describe Heidi's relationship with Grandmamma.
2. What results because of Heidi's realization in the third quote above?
3. How has being able to read made a difference in Heidi's life?
4. Why do you think the story about the shepherd is Heidi's favorite?

Enrichment

1. First impressions are important. Often the first impression we give of ourselves when meeting someone new is the way they always think of us. Directions: Write about your first impression of Grandmamma from the chapter. Did your opinion of her change or stay the same throughout the chapter? Give at least two examples to support your answer.

Answers will vary.

Reading Notes

mortar — a mixture of lime or cement with sand and water used as a bonding agent between bricks, stones, etc.

excursion — a short trip or outing

Vocabulary

Write the meaning of each bold word or phrase.

1. she cried, **penitently**: "I will ask God to forgive me …" feeling sorry for sin or wrongdoing
2. The children felt quite **forlorn**. lonely and sad
3. The effort it cost her produced such queer **grimaces**. painful facial expressions
4. She looked very thin and **peaky**. sickly; pale

Comprehension Questions

Answer the following in complete sentences.

1. What are the pleasant distractions that cannot cure Heidi's homesickness?
   They try sewing doll's clothes and reading stories, but Heidi's eyes don't sparkle.

2. What is Heidi missing in her attempt at prayer? Trust and faith are missing.

3. How does the attempted remedy to soothe the girls' sadness over Grandmamma's departure make things worse? Heidi volunteers to read a story to Clara, but the story they read is about a grandmother dying. This causes Heidi to weep as she thinks about the possibility of Grannie dying.

4. What does Miss Rottenmeier threaten because of Heidi's crying? What is the effect on Heidi?
   She threatens to take the book away. Heidi will do anything to keep it so she never weeps again while reading.

Quotations

The day of Grandmamma's departure was a sad one for Clara and Heidi, but she managed to keep them happy right up to the moment when she drove off in the carriage. It was only when the sounds of the wheels died away, and the house was so quiet and empty, that the children felt quite forlorn and did not know what to do with themselves.

Heidi's homesickness grew on her from day to day, till just reading the name of some well-loved object was enough to bring tears to her eyes, though she would not let them fall.

Discussion Questions

1. Why does Heidi stop praying to God?
2. Explain Grandmamma's answer to Heidi's disillusionment about unanswered prayer.
3. Read the first quote above. Have you ever had an experience like this? What did you do to ease the loneliness?
4. What are possible solutions to cure Heidi's homesickness in the second quote?

Enrichment

1. Heidi learns to sew in this chapter by sewing clothes for her dolls. With a parent, sew an outfit for a doll, stuffed animal, or figurine.
2. Copy, or write from dictation, the paragraph that begins with "Clara had great difficulty in persuading her …".

Clara had great difficulty in persuading her that the story was about quite another grandmother, and even when she began to understand that, she was not comforted for it had made her realize that Peter's Grannie might really die, and her grandfather too, while she was so far away, and that if she did not go home for a long time, she might arrive to find everything changed and her loved ones gone for ever.

Reading Notes

booty something that is taken by violence and robbery
portly heavy, overweight, stout
draught British spelling of "draft"
forebears ancestors, forefathers

Vocabulary

Write the meaning of each bold word or phrase.

1. a bottle of wine to **fortify** them. to strengthen
2. He settled himself more comfortably at each effort to **rouse** him. to awaken
3. It was not possible for him to return home so **precipitately.** suddenly
4. "The child's not **robust**." strong and healthy

Comprehension Questions

Answer the following in complete sentences.

1. How do Sebastian and John respond to seeing the "ghost"? John is frightened and runs back into the room, slamming and locking the door behind them. They do not leave the room until it is daylight outside.

2. What is Miss Rottenmeier's reaction to Sebastian and John's observation? She is very frightened and writes to Mr. Sesemann at once, asking him to return immediately.

3. What is Miss Rottenmeier's idea to get Mr. Sesemann to take notice? Does it work? She tells Clara of the "ghost," knowing it will frighten her and that that will get Mr. Sesemann's attention. It works.

4. What is Heidi's recurring dream? Is it related to the front door's mysterious nightly opening? She dreams of going to the door of Grandfather's hut to look outside and see the stars. When she has this dream, she sleepwalks downstairs and opens the front door.

Quotations

"The front door was wide open and there was a white figure on the stairs which suddenly vanished."

Who said this? John To whom? Sebastian

"Fright might even send her into fits or bring on an attack of St. Vitus' dance."

Who wrote this? Miss Rottenmeier To whom? Mr. Sesemann

"I must ask you not to cast reflections on my entirely respectable forebears!"

Who said this? Mr. Sesemann To whom? Miss Rottenmeier

"This is not an illness that can be cured with pills and powders. The child's not robust …"

Who said this? Dr. Classen To whom? Mr. Sesemann

Discussion Questions

1. Mr. Sesemann has the doctor come and help him watch for the "ghost." Who or what does Mr. Sesemann think is responsible for the appearances?
2. How is the first vigil for the ghost different from the second?
3. What is the scene depicted in the chapter's illustration?

Enrichment

1. In the second quote above, Miss Rottenmeier states that Clara could be susceptible to an attack of "St. Vitus' dance." Read the description of the illness in the Appendix.
2. Dr. Classen diagnoses Heidi's problem. Write a paragraph answering the following questions: What is his diagnosis? Do you think it will be effective? Why or why not? Give at least two supporting reasons as to whether or not you think it will be effective.

   Dr. Classen says that Heidi is terribly homesick, she has lost a lot of weight, and her nerves are in a bad state. She needs to go home right away. Answers will vary.

Reading Notes

precipices cliffs with very steep drop-offs or overhangs
of her own accord by her own decision

Vocabulary

Write the meaning of each bold word or phrase.

1. They sped to the dining-room, all rather **dishevelled**. untidy; disorderly
2. "Please do excuse me," she said **glibly**. insincerely
3. "Oh yes, I am," she said **fervently**, and colour came into her cheeks. having great enthusiasm or spirit
4. She gave him an **imploring** look. desperately begging

Comprehension Questions

Answer the following in complete sentences.

1. What does Clara do that shows she is a person of her word? She makes sure the rolls are ready for Grannie, as promised.
2. What is the last mean thing Miss Rottenmeier does to Heidi? Who defends her? She scolds Heidi and tries to take away the old hat and red scarf. Mr. Sesemann lets her take it with her.
3. What does Sebastian do to indicate he is used to city living and is out of his "comfort zone" in the mountain area? He is afraid to climb up the mountain and doesn't think the roads are safe.
4. Why do the townspeople think Heidi returned? Who brings the truth to light? They think the only reason she would return is because she's been treated badly. The baker tells them she has been homesick.
5. What reason does Heidi have for not wearing the dignified, fine plumage hat? She remembers her grandfather had said he never wanted to see her in a feathered hat.

Quotations

Mr. Sesemann saw through her excuses, and sent her away without another word.

Who did Mr. Sesemann send away? Detie

"I'd a million times rather be with Grandfather on the mountain than anywhere else in the world."

Who said this? Heidi To whom? the baker

It was so lovely, Heidi stood with tears pouring down her cheeks, and thanked God for letting her come home to it again.

Discussion Questions

1. In the first quote above, why do you think Mr. Sesemann allows her to leave without any discussion?
2. When Grandfather and Heidi first see each other again, he is unable to speak and has tears in his eyes for the first time in many years. When he does speak again he doesn't say how he feels about Heidi's return. Based on his actions, how do you think he feels about Heidi coming back?
3. Grandfather reads the letter from Mr. Sesemann, puts it in his pocket, and doesn't say anything about it. What do you think the letter says? Why would he not say anything?

Enrichment

1. In this chapter, Heidi returns home after having been away for some time. Write about a time when you came home after having been away on a trip, at camp, or for a visit to someone else's house. How did you feel upon coming back to your own familiar surroundings?
2. Copy, or write from dictation, the last paragraph of the chapter. Watch spelling and punctuation.

During the night Uncle Alp went up to the loft at least ten times to make sure she was all right, and to see that the round hole in the wall was still stopped with hay to prevent the moonlight shining on her face. But Heidi did not stir. She slept soundly all night long, satisfied through and through. She was home again. She had seen the sun setting on the mountains. She had heard the wind whistling through the fir trees.

THE PLEIADES

By day you cannot see the sky
For it is up so very high.
You look and look, but it's so blue
That you can never see right through.

But when night comes it is quite plain,
And all the stars are there again.
They seem just like old friends to me,
I've known them all my life you see.

There is the dipper first, and there
Is Cassiopeia in her chair,
Orion's belt, the Milky Way,
And lots I know but cannot say.

One group looks like a swarm of bees,
Papa says they're the Pleiades;
But I think they must be the toy
Of some nice little angel boy.

Perhaps his jackstones which today
He has forgot to put away,
And left them lying on the sky
Where he will find them bye and bye.

I wish he'd come and play with me.
We'd have such fun, for it would be
A most unusual thing for boys
To feel that they had stars for toys!

—Amy Lowell

Poetry Link!

Use the following questions to discuss the poem.

1. How many syllables are in each line? Write the number at the end of each line.
   8
2. Where do the rhymes occur?
   at the end of every two lines
3. How are stars like old friends?
   They are always around, so they are very familiar.
4. What is referred to by "the dipper"?
   the 2 constellations - the big dipper and the little dipper
5. List each constellation mentioned.
   Cassiopeia, the dippers, Orion's belt, the Pleiades
6. Describe the imagery found in the fourth stanza.
   The Pleiades looks like a swarm of bees or a little angel boy's jacks.
7. What are jackstones?
   We call them jacks—a children's game.
8. Who is the speaker/ voice of the poem?
   a boy - "a most unusual thing for boys …"
9. What story does the author create to explain the stars?
   A little boy is looking at the stars and recognizes them as old friends. He names them and imagines playing with them.

Copy "The Pleiades" below.

Reading Notes

copper penny

beckon to signal or summon with a gesture of the head or hand

Vocabulary

Write the meaning of each bold word or phrase.

1. such a peaceful expression on Grannie's **careworn** face. worried
2. and now everything looked **spick and span**. very clean
3. If God **forsakes** a man, that's final. abandons
4. The **prospect** of Grandmamma coming expectation or looking forward

Comprehension Questions

Answer the following in complete sentences.

1. What actions and statements of Heidi's demonstrate her generous nature? She gives her hat to Bridget and decides to spend her money on bread for Grannie. She would rather give Grannie rolls than have a new bed.
2. What has Heidi come to realize about her relationship with God and her prayer life? She learned a great deal from Grandmamma and now knows that God knows best when to give her what she needs. She realizes that patience is important.
3. How do the townspeople respond to Uncle Alp's visits to church and the parsonage? At church, everyone watches him with interest. They wonder if he will be angry or friendly after visiting the pastor. They notice how gently he holds Heidi's hand.
4. What evidence indicates that the townspeople have a change of heart? They begin to talk of the good deeds they have heard of Grandfather doing. When Grandfather leaves the parsonage everyone is eager to shake his hand and invite them into their homes. They look forward to when he will join them in the winter.
5. What arrives that is exciting to Peter? Why does its arrival cause such excitement? He delivers a letter to Heidi and finds it exciting because no one in his house ever receives letters.

Quotations

"God knew what was best, just as Clara's Grandmamma said He did, and see how perfectly He arranged everything."

Who said this? Heidi To whom? Grandfather

"You see, today I am happy, as I had never thought to be again. Much happier than I deserve. It's good to feel at peace with God and man. It was a good day when God sent you to me."

Who said this? Grandfather To whom? Heidi

Discussion Questions

1. In the first quote above, what are some examples Heidi gives of how God knew what was best?
2. The parallel to the story of the prodigal son reappears in this chapter. What significance does the story have for Grandfather?
3. Sometimes in stories the setting is a reflection of the characters' moods. Describe the setting of Sunday morning and tell how it might reflect Grandfather's and Heidi's moods.
4. In the second quote above, we see Grandfather at peace with God and man. What has he done to reach this place of peace?

Enrichment

1. Heidi receives a letter from Clara. Read what Clara wrote and then compose a letter from Heidi responding to Clara's letter. Use the format for a friendly letter (you can make up the date and address—just try to make it realistic based on what we know from the story). Be sure to include correct punctuation and capitalization.

1 Alpine Way
Dorfli, Switzerland 50789
June 5, 1880

Dear Clara,

Responses will vary.

Your friend,
Heidi

Reading Notes

decorum dignified, polite behavior
practicable capable of being done

Vocabulary

Write the meaning of each bold word or phrase.

1. Mr. Sesemann listened at first with a **resigned** expression. accepting or unresisting
2. The doctor laughed a little **wryly.** amused at something contrary or ironi
3. Clara quite expected to have a **tussle** with Miss Rottenmeier. disagreement
4. Servants have a remarkable **faculty** of knowing what is going on. ability; skill

Comprehension Questions

Answer the following in complete sentences.

1. Why isn't Clara going to visit Heidi? Clara has been too ill to travel, and the trip would most likely only make her condition worse.

2. Who goes in Clara's place to visit Heidi? Is the substitute a good choice? The doctor decides to go and represent the family, at Mr. Sesemann's suggestion. Clara is satisfied with the choice.

3. What influences the doctor to make the journey to visit Heidi? Mr. Sesemann talks him into it, thinking it will help with his sadness over the death of his daughter. Clara also promises to take cod liver oil and wants a report about Heidi.

4. What can be said about the doctor's ability to deal with Miss Rottenmeier? He knows how to put her at ease and is able to flatter her to get her to do what he wants.

5. List all the things that are put in the parcel and who they are for. There is a coat and assorted little surprises for Heidi, a shawl and cakes for Grannie, a sausage for Peter's family, and pipe tobacco for Grandfather.

Quotations

"Even if she does miss much, she's still better off than many children. Count your blessings. Remember how lucky you are to have each other."

Who said this? Dr. Classen To whom? Mr. Sesemann

Servants have a remarkable faculty of knowing what is going on in a house, long before they are actually told, and Sebastian and Tinette were particularly good at it.

Discussion Questions

1. What is the context for the first quote? Do you think this is good encouragement, given the circumstances? Why or why not?
2. In the second quote above, how do you think the servants know before being told?
3. Clara packs many gifts for Heidi and those she loves. Discuss each gift and how it demonstrates Clara's thoughtfulness.
4. Clara's character shines through in this chapter. Give specific character traits you have observed and examples from the story.

Enrichment

1. Copy, or write from dictation, the paragraph that begins, "Clara could not keep the tears from her eyes …".

Clara could not keep the tears from her eyes though she knew her father hated to see her cry, but it was very hard to have to give up the visit to Heidi, for she had counted on it all through the long and lonely hours of her illness. But her father would never have disappointed her unless he thought it important for her good, she knew that, so she blinked back the tears and turned to the doctor.

Reading Notes

at full tilt	at fastest speed
robbed him of his speech	made unable to speak

Vocabulary

Write the meaning of each bold word or phrase.

1. The brown goat got too **boisterous**. noisy
2. Daisy stood a little **aloof** at a distance
3. They greeted her in their own **obstreperous** fashion noisy and disorderly

Comprehension Questions

Answer the following in complete sentences.

1. How did Heidi's stay at Frankfurt affect her habits and ideas about housekeeping? She learned to keep everything neat and tidy every single day.

2. What distracts Heidi while she is doing her housework? Heidi is distracted by many different things: sunbeams, the beauty of the scenery, and the fir trees' song.

3. What specific things does Heidi do to "chase the shadow from the doctor's eyes"? She holds his hand and tells him summer will soon come.

4. What makes Heidi speechless with excitement? Heidi is amazed at the package of gifts Clara has sent.

5. What is Bridget's reaction to the present given to her and her family? She looks at it reverently because it is more than they have ever had before.

Quotations

"Oh, it will soon be spring. Time goes quickly up here. They'll be able to stay longer then, and Clara will like that."

Who said this? Heidi To whom? Dr. Classen

"This is certainly the place for Clara to come to. She would soon become a different person if she could eat as I have today, and get quite plump and rosy."

Who said this? Dr. Classen To whom? Heidi and Grandfather

Discussion Questions

1. What is the scene depicted in the chapter's illustration?
2. Heidi is really disappointed that Clara and Grandmamma cannot come. How does she respond to the disappointment? Have you ever experienced similar disappointment? How did you respond?

Enrichment

1. Every morning Grandfather goes outside and looks around "to see what kind of day it was going to be." From ancient times people have been trying to predict what is going to happen with the weather. Research different kinds of weather forecasting and determine what type Grandfather uses.
2. Heidi has new habits regarding her daily chores. Use the chapter's description to make a "to-do" list for Heidi on the paper below.

Make bed
Fold clothes
Tidy hut
Move chairs
Polish table

Reading Notes

made amends righted a wrong
crevice a narrow crack or opening
pell-mell recklessly hurried

Vocabulary

Write the meaning of each bold word or phrase.

1. A **fleeting** smile crossed his face. temporary; passing quickly
2. He kicked the turf and **scowled.** frowned and glared
3. They saw the great bird rise up, protesting, at their **intrusion**. unwelcome arrival

Comprehension Questions

Answer the following in complete sentences.

1. How does Peter act toward the doctor? How do you account for these actions? Peter is very begrudging of the doctor's presence. Out of jealousy, he acts hatefully toward him but then is sorry for doing so and tries to make private amends.

2. What words of wisdom does Heidi give the doctor? What is the role reversal of the conversation? She tells him to trust God. In Frankfurt it was Grandmamma and the doctor who comforted Heidi. Here, she is taking the "adult" role and comforting the doctor.

3. How does the hymn affect the doctor? It reminds him of his happy childhood and of pleasing memories of his mother.

4. What does Heidi promise the doctor as he is leaving the mountains? Heidi promises to come to Frankfurt to care for the doctor if he is ever ill or lonely.

Quotations

"Can you understand that even up here it is possible for sorrow to cast a shadow over the eyes so that one can't really enjoy the beauty, and that adds to the sadness?"

Who said this? the doctor To whom? Heidi

The weather was fine and sunny all that month, and the doctor came up to the hut every morning, and from there went off on long walks, often with Uncle Alp as his companion.

Discussion Questions

1. What kinds of things do Grandfather and the doctor see on their long walks?
2. What makes Heidi volunteer to return to Frankfurt at the end of the chapter? Why is she encouraged to stay?
3. What clues help the reader predict that the doctor might someday return to Dorfli?

Enrichment

1. This chapter mentions some mountain peaks having "eternal snows." Research how the snow is able to last year-round on some peaks.
2. The author describes Heidi's favorite spot on the mountains in the beginning of the chapter. Use the description to draw a picture of the view.
3. Copy, or write from dictation, the paragraph that begins, "Heidi sat pondering for a while." Watch for spelling and punctuation.

   Heidi sat pondering for a while. She was sure God could always help, but was trying to find the answer out of her own experiences. "I think you have to wait," she said at last, "and keep on thinking that God has something good which He's going to give you out of the sad thing, but you have to be patient. You see, when something's awfully bad, you don't know about the good bit coming, and you think it's going on for ever."

THE NIGHTINGALE AND THE GLOW-WORM

A nightingale, that all day long
Had cheered the village with his song,
Nor yet at eve his note suspended,
Nor yet when eventide was ended,
Began to feel—as well he might—
The keen demands of appetite;
When, looking eagerly around,
He spied, far off, upon the ground,
A something shining in the dark,
And knew the glow-worm by his spark;
So, stooping down from hawthorn top,
He thought to put him in his crop.
The worm, aware of his intent,
Harangued him thus, quite eloquent—
"Did you admire my lamp," quoth he,
"As much as I your minstrelsy,
You would abhor to do me wrong,
As much as I to spoil your song;
For 'twas the self-same Power divine
Taught you to sing, and me to shine;
That you with music, I with light,
Might beautify and cheer the night."
The songster heard his short oration,
And, warbling out his approbation,
Released him, as my story tells,
And found a supper somewhere else.

—William Cowper

Poetry Link!

Use the following questions to discuss the poem.

1. Why does the author include the word "nor"? What does it mean?
   "Nor" means "and not" or "or not." The author probably thinks it is more poetic sounding than saying "and not."
2. Define "eventide."
   evening
3. Define "keen."
   sharp; strong
4. What is the hawthorn top?
   the top of a hawthorn tree
5. What does "harangued" mean?
   a tirade; a speech characterized by strong meaning
6. Who is the "self-same Power divine"?
   God
7. What is the argument used to convince the nightingale to sacrifice the glow-worm?
   The glow-worm points out that his gift of light is just as valuable as the nightingale's gift of song, and so he should be spared so he can continue to bless the world with his light.
8. How many syllables are there per line? Write the number at the end of each line.
   8
9. Where do the rhymes occur?
   at the end of every two lines

Copybook

Copy "The Nightingale and the Glow-Worm" below.

Reading Notes

barricade any barrier that blocks passage
parsonage minister's home
partition something that separates or divides

Vocabulary

Write the meaning of each bold word or phrase.

1. only Peter was **agile** enough to squeeze through. quick in movement
2. Heidi understood Peter's **cryptic** remark perfectly. mysterious
3. "That's **desertion**," said Uncle Alp, "and deserters get punished." leaving one's duty without permission

Comprehension Questions

Answer the following in complete sentences.

1. What is Peter's decision regarding school attendance? What excuses are used for his absenteeism? Peter finds any excuse to avoid school which he doesn't like, until Uncle Alp threatens to beat him for non-attendance. Excuses include these: snow was too deep, sled took him too far, it was too late in the day.

2. What is the analogy of Heidi's experience in Frankfurt and the goats' new stall? The goats are as unhappy in their new stall that first day as Heidi had been in Frankfurt, a fact which Grandfather points out.

3. What is Grannie's secret worry? Grannie is worried that someone will take Heidi back to Frankfurt and she will never see her again.

4. What does Heidi discover when she steps foot into Peter's hut? Grannie isn't at her spinning wheel; she is sick in bed.

Quotation

Lying in her comfortable bed behind the stove that night, Heidi thought about Grannie's poor thin pillow, and how much good the hymns had done her. If she could go and read to her every day, Grannie might get better, but it would probably be a week or even longer before she could go up again.

Discussion Questions

1. How does Grandfather cause Peter to understand the true nature of his "desertion"?
2. Compare and contrast Peter and Heidi's views of school.
3. Heidi wants Grannie to be able to hear her hymns every day, but she can't go because of the snow. What are possible solutions to this problem?

Enrichment

1. Peter is often truant from school, and his teacher does not do anything about it. In the United States, there are laws concerning school attendance. Find out what the truancy laws are in your state or area.
2. Use the blank space below to draw a blueprint of the ramshackle house in which Heidi and Uncle Alp spend the winter in Dorfli. Use the description in the chapter as your guide. Include doors and prominent features mentioned.

Reading Notes

forthwith immediately, right away

keen eager, interested, enthusiastic

Vocabulary

Write the meaning of each bold word or phrase.

1. "I don't believe that any more," she told him **squarely**. directly; straightforwardly
2. After his **exertions**, Peter was usually invited to stay to supper. hard work
3. Peter was **bewildered** by all these threats of trouble. confused
4. He was inclined to be **cocky**. feeling too proud of oneself

Comprehension Questions

Answer the following in complete sentences.

1. What hurdle does Heidi have to overcome before Peter can read? Peter is convinced that he can't read, so Heidi first has to get him past his stubbornness on the subject.

2. How does Heidi get Peter to agree to let her teach him to read? She tells him how terrible life would be in the school in Frankfurt which his mother threatened to send him to—in essence frightening or threatening him into agreeing.

3. How does Heidi describe what school would be like in Frankfurt? What kind of school is it? It is probably a boys' boarding school. Heidi describes the teachers as very harsh and intimidating. She tells Peter that the other boys would mock him for not being able to read.

4. What techniques does Heidi use to help Peter learn and remember his letters? She uses rhymes, imagery, and lots of repetition to help him remember.

5. How does the teacher react to hearing that Peter has learned to read? He asks if a miracle has occurred.

Quotations

"I don't believe that any more and nor does anyone else. Clara's Grandmamma told me it wasn't so and she was right."

Who said this? Heidi To whom? Peter

The truth was that Peter made things as easy as possible for himself. When he came to a difficult word, he just left it out, thinking that a few words less among so many would make no difference to Grannie. Consequently there was sometimes little sense in what he read.

Discussion Questions

1. What is Heidi referring to in the first quote? Do you think your attitude about an issue can affect how well you do it? Why?
2. What is Peter's reaction to the rhymes Heidi uses?
3. What is Uncle Alp's reaction to the lessons?
4. What does the second quote tell you about Peter? Have you noticed this in him before?

Enrichment

1. In this chapter Heidi is intensely curious as to the whereabouts of the Hottentots. Read Appendix II to find out more about the Hottentots.
2. Copy, or write from dictation, the second to last paragraph in the chapter. Watch spelling and punctuation.

Once Grannie replied to her, "Yes, I'm glad for his sake that he has learnt something. But I shall be thankful when the spring is here, and Heidi can come again. They are somehow not the same hymns when Peter reads them, and I keep trying to fill in the gaps, and so I miss what comes next. So they don't do me as much good as when Heidi reads them."

Reading Notes

hither and thither	here and there
haunt	a place frequently visited
centaury	pink-petaled plant
ado	busy activity; bustle; fuss

Vocabulary

Write the meaning of each bold word or phrase.

1. Peter went after them **brandishing** the stick. waving
2. This one you're in must be a **trifle** hard. a little bit; small amount
3. Foresight is a virtue and **averts** many a misfortune. to ward off or prevent

Comprehension Questions

Answer the following in complete sentences.

1. Why doesn't Miss Rottenmeier join the group of travelers? She is afraid of the mountains because of Sebastian's descriptions of them.

2. Compare Heidi's and Peter's feelings about more visitors coming from Frankfurt.
Heidi is overjoyed, but Peter is angry and jealous.

3. What does Heidi say that convinces Grannie that her fears are warranted?
Heidi tells her she doesn't want what is best for her if Grannie won't survive it. Grannie misunderstands this statement.

4. Describe the procession climbing the hill.
Two men carry Clara in a chair on poles, another leads the horse Grandmamma rides, and two more men push the wheelchair and carry a big bundle.

5. What is the loveliest moment of the day for Clara?
At night in the hayloft, Clara is able to look at the starry sky.

Quotations

She stood admiring them, thinking how long they must have stood there looking down on the valley below, while generation after generation of men came and went, were born and died, and they stood fast, for ever stretching upwards to the sky.

What is this quote about? the fir trees behind the hut

"Then you come out with an offer which solves the whole problem, and as though it were the easiest thing in the world. I can't thank you enough."

Who said this? Grandmamma To whom? Uncle Alp

"Foresight is a virtue and averts many a misfortune."

Who said this? Grandmamma

Discussion Questions

1. This chapter discloses some information about Uncle Alp's past. What do we learn about his former life? Does it fit with the story Detie told at the beginning?
2. What does Clara think of Heidi's home and the mountains?
3. What is being referred to in the second quote? Why does the speaker appreciate the offer?
4. What is foresight? How does it avert misfortune? Do you have any examples from your experience where foresight has averted misfortune?

Enrichment

1. Check out a book on flowers from the library and look for pictures of the flowers mentioned in this chapter. Draw a picture of your findings on a separate page.
2. Heidi is overjoyed to have Clara and Grandmamma come visit her. Write a paragraph about a time when you had a special visitor in your home. Tell what kinds of preparations you made for their coming and how you felt upon their arrival.

Answers will vary.

Vocabulary

Write the meaning of each bold word or phrase.

1. quietly watching the mists **disperse** over the mountains to spread out or scatter
2. By his time she had managed to **extricate** herself from the goats. to untangle
3. Heidi longed to see it so **passionately** showing strong feeling
4. Clara, too, was excited at the thought of such an **expedition**. trip; voyage

Comprehension Questions

Answer the following in complete sentences.

1. How does Uncle Alp hide the wheelchair when it doesn't fit through the door of the hut?
   He removes boards from the shed so it can be pushed inside under cover.
2. What do the girls do their first morning together? They compose letters to Grandmamma while sitting outside.
3. What is Uncle Alp's special treat for the girls? He brings them mugs filled with goat's milk and bread spread with butter.
4. Why do you think it hurts Clara to stand on her legs at first? How does Uncle Alp help?
   She is so unaccustomed to using her legs that the first try is painful. Uncle Alp supports her and gives her daily practice, asking for a little more time each day.
5. What incentive does Grandfather use to help Clara? Grandfather will take them up to the pasture with the goats if Clara will try to stand alone.

Quotations

"Now why are you staring over there, as if you wanted to eat somebody? They won't interfere with you."

Who said this? Grandfather To whom? Peter

"As long as I can remember I've only eaten because I had to. Everything always tasted so of cod-liver oil, and I used to wish I didn't have to eat at all. And here, I can hardly wait for your grandfather to bring my milk."

Who said this? Clara To whom? Heidi

Uncle Alp grew very attached to his little guest and tried to find something new every day to make her better.

Discussion Questions

1. What is the context of the first quote? Why does the person look as though they "wanted to eat somebody"?
2. What does the third quote tell us about Grandfather? Tell some examples of things he does to make Clara better.

Enrichment

1. Throughout the book, the mountains represent a place of healing and restoration. Both Heidi and Dr. Classen are rejuvenated on the mountain. In this chapter Uncle Alp wants Clara to try to stay outside all day to benefit her health. Spend an afternoon or a day outside among nature and enjoy God's creation!
2. Copy, or write from dictation, the paragraph that begins, "When Clara had been there a fortnight ...". Watch spelling and punctuation.

    When Clara had been there a fortnight Uncle Alp began trying to get her on her feet each morning, before putting her in her chair. "Won't the little one try to stand for a minute?" he asked gently, and to please him, she did try, but gave up very quickly because it hurt her, and she clung to him for support. But each day he persuaded her to try for a little longer.

Reading Notes

rascal a mischievous person

sorrel any plant in the buckwheat family with acid-flavored leaves, used in salads or sauces

Vocabulary

Write the meaning of each bold word or phrase.

1. His **resentment** got too much for him. anger at something; bitterness
2. Heidi gazed **ecstatically** at the yellow carpet of rock-roses. with joyful excitement
3. Clara was able to sit among all the **profusion** of beautiful flowers. a great amount

Comprehension Questions

Answer the following in complete sentences.

1. Onto what object does Peter project all his anger and jealousy? What action indicates his built up rage? The wheelchair receives all of Peter's pent-up feelings. He pushes the wheelchair down the hill to Dorfli in rebellion against Clara.
2. What is one theory behind the destruction of the wheelchair? One theory offered is that it was blown over by the wind.
3. What strange new experience is Clara enjoying when Heidi goes to the flower meadow? Clara is feeding Snowflake, the goat, and is able to enjoy the beauty around her. She feels almost like a normal girl.
4. Why does Peter help Heidi with Clara so she can experience the flower meadow? He is afraid Heidi knows he has destroyed the wheelchair and will tell her grandfather.
5. Why does Heidi believe you should pray to God even though He already knows everything you need and want? Praying to God shows that we know He is in control and that we trust Him with all areas of our life. It is a recognition of God's provision for us.

Quotations

The real badness of what he had done had not yet occurred to him, nor any idea of what consequences it might have.

This quote refers to whom? Peter

She had never expected to know such happiness, and it gave her a new idea of what it must mean to be like other girls, well and free, to run about and to help people, instead of always having to be the one that sat still and was waited on.

This quote refers to whom? Clara

"Something attempted, something won."

Who said this? Grandfather To whom? Clara

Discussion Questions

1. What are the consequences the person in the first quote experiences?
2. According to the second quote, why does Clara desire to be well? What does this tell you about her?
3. What is meant by the third quote?
4. Uncle Alp finds several things about the wheelchair's destruction to be unusual. Tell what observations he makes. Do you think he knows Peter destroyed it? Why?

Enrichment

1. The girls compose a letter to Grandmamma inviting her to the mountains. Write the salutation, body, and closing of the letter below in the way you think Heidi and Clara would have written it.

Answers will vary.

Reading Notes

pace	the distance covered in a step
goad	a stick with a pointed end for moving cattle; prod
giddy	lighthearted

Vocabulary

Write the meaning of each bold word or phrase.

1. A man with a **laden** basket brought up the rear. loaded down; burdened
2. hastily **improvising** a welcome. to make or do something at the spur of the moment
3. "Oh how **exquisite**!" she cried. exceptionally fine
4. and he came slowly towards her with an **agonized** expression. painful
5. Uncle had spoken with **conviction**. firm belief

Comprehension Questions

Answer the following in complete sentences.

1. What is weighing heavily on Peter's mind as the days go on and on? He is feeling guilty about destroying the wheelchair and is afraid that the policeman from Frankfurt will come for him at any time.
2. What makes Mrs. Sesemann's anxiety turn to astonishment? Mrs. Sesemann is anxious about the absence of a wheelchair, but Clara looks so healthy that she is hardly recognizable. And then she stands and walks!
3. Why does Uncle Alp whistle for Peter? What does Peter think the whistling means? He whistles for Peter so the telegram can be carried to town. Peter expects to be arrested.
4. Who does Peter think Mr. Sesemann is when he runs into him down the path? He thinks Mr. Sesemann is a policeman.
5. After reading the whole story, what can be said about Heidi's and Clara's friendship? Their friendship was very strong, and would probably last a lifetime. They had learned a great deal from one another.

Quotations

"Oh Papa, if you only knew all that Uncle Alp has done for me! I shall never forget it. And I keep thinking, what could I ever do for him that would give him even half as much pleasure as he has given me?"

Who said this? Clara

"Heidi's going to stay here with you. We know what a comfort she is to you. We shall want to see her too, of course, but we shall come to her. We shall come every year to the mountains to give thanks for our child's wonderful recovery."

Who said this? Grandmamma To whom? Grannie

Discussion Questions

1. How does Mrs. Sesemann respond to Peter's confession of pushing the wheelchair over the mountain? Do you agree or disagree? Why?
2. This chapter holds the resolution to many different problems/conflicts that appear throughout the book. Try to list as many resolutions found in this chapter as possible. Discuss their significance.

Enrichment

1. The Sesemanns once again show their generosity in this chapter. Make a list of the gifts given and their recipients below.

RECIPIENT	GIFT
Peter	penny a week for life
Grannie	new bed, warm clothes
Grandfather	Heidi will be taken care of
Heidi	the bed for Grannie

2. Write a paragraph about your favorite chapter from *Heidi*. Give at least three detailed reasons for why it is your favorite.

Answers will vary.

Appendix I

St. Vitus' Dance refers to a disease that causes involuntary movements of the arms, legs and face. It can last for 2-6 months and will often end on its own. It mostly affects children and is more common in girls than in boys. St. Vitus has his name attached to it because he is the patron saint of dance. It seems that it would be highly unlikely that Clara would develop this disease from fright; the disease is usually associated with rheumatic fever.

Appendix II

The Hottentots are a tribe from Southern Africa. Dutch settlers gave the tribe the name Hottentot in reference to their language which included clicking sounds. The Hottentots call themselves "Khoikhoi" or "Khoekhoe," which roughly translates as "men of men."

Discussion Questions Answer Key

Chapter 1

1. What does the first quote above tell us about Detie's character? Do you agree or disagree with her analysis of the situation? Why?

   Detie is more concerned with her personal advancement than she is Heidi's welfare. Answers will vary.

2. The author tells us that Detie is "... really far from easy in her mind about what she [is] doing ..." What are the reasons for her uneasiness?

   Detie had promised her mother (Heidi's maternal grandmother) that she would look after the child. The townspeople's denouncement of her actions also makes her uneasy. It is also possible that she knows on some level that what she is doing is not right.

3. What does it mean to be "at odds with God and man"? What are the reasons for Uncle Alp choosing this lifestyle?

   "At odds with God and man" means that the relationships Uncle Alp had with God and others has been strained almost to the point of breaking. He made many foolish decisions that caused others harm. As far as we can tell, he did not seek reconciliation after the harm had been done and people are hardened against him. He felt everyone was against him and so he escaped up to the mountain where he does not have to come in contact with people.

4. With what we know about Uncle Alp and Heidi so far, how do you think Heidi and Uncle Alp are going to get along?

   Answers will vary, but from what we know, it does not look promising.

Chapter 2

1. In the first quote above and throughout the chapter, Heidi watches Grandfather with great interest. Find two other places in the chapter where Heidi observes Grandfather and tell why you think she does so.

   1) She watches him do his chores after dinner.
   2) She observes him making her a high chair.
   3) She watches him as he makes small repairs on the hut.
   Answers will vary; she is interested in what he is doing in part because this is all new to her. Heidi is naturally curious and enjoys learning.

2. In this chapter, Heidi proves herself to be willing to work. Give examples supporting this statement.

   She puts away her bundle of clothes. Heidi helps Grandfather make her bed. She helps her grandfather get ready for their afternoon meal.

3. Do you think the townspeople are correct or incorrect in their thoughts about Uncle Alp (from Chapter 1)? Why? Give examples of specific actions to support your opinion.

   Answers will vary; just be sure the actions clearly support the opinion.

4. There are two illustrations in this chapter. Describe what is occurring in each picture.

   The first picture illustrates the point in the chapter where Heidi has explored her new surroundings and comes back to Grandfather to ask to see the inside of the hut. The second picture shows Heidi and Grandfather making her bed.

Chapter 3

1. The quotes above show the creative way Grandfather explains everyday events to Heidi. Why does Grandfather explain things in this way? Think of some examples of this from your own experience and discuss.

    Grandfather explains the events in a way that a child Heidi's age can understand. Answers will vary.

2. What does the third quote above tell you about Uncle Alp?

    The hawk and Uncle Alp are similar in his mind. He thinks that is what the hawk is saying because that is how he feels about things. He thinks it is better to be left alone and away from people and, therefore, so does the hawk.

3. Heidi feels a special bond with Snowflake. What are the reasons for this bond?

    Snowflake is an orphan like Heidi and so she feels the need to care for her. Snowflake also readily accepts Heidi's kindness.

Chapter 4

1. What clues does the author give that Peter's Grannie is blind?

    Grannie feels for Heidi's hand. She asks Bridget if Heidi came the way of Uncle Alp. Grannie asks Bridget what Heidi looks like.

2. What is your opinion of Uncle Alp's response to Bridget (4th quote above)?

    Answers will vary.

3. Contrast Grannie's outlook on life before and after Heidi starts to visit. How does the third quote above relate to your answer?

    Before Heidi's visits, Grannie felt hopeless, was sad, and couldn't wait until the days were over. After Heidi starts to visit she feels hopeful and happy. She thinks the afternoons now go by too fast.

Chapter 5

1. Contrast Grandfather's view of formal schooling with the pastor's.

    He doesn't want school to teach Heidi bad ideas. He believes Heidi will be happy in nature. The pastor believes Heidi should attend school to learn to read and write.

2. Contrast Detie's view of the goats to Heidi's.

    Detie thinks them stupid and obstinate and believes Heidi has learned this behavior from them. For Heidi, they have become her unique and special friends.

3. What is your opinion of Detie taking Heidi to Frankfurt?

    Answers will vary.

4. How does Heidi's leaving affect Grandfather? Grannie?

    Grandfather is clearly very upset. He becomes more withdrawn and angry. For Grannie, the days become long and sad. She wishes to see Heidi again before she dies.

Chapter 6

1. What character traits does Detie exhibit in her encounter with Miss Rottenmeier?

   Determination, spirit, cunningness, quickness, ingenuity

2. What are possible solutions to Miss Rottenmeier's problem in the second quote?

   Possible answers could include: have Detie take Heidi back to Grandfather, find another home for her, allow Heidi to stay, etc.

3. What is the scene depicted in the chapter's illustration? Try to identify the characters using clues from the chapter to help you.

   It is the first meeting between Heidi and the Sesemann household.

Chapter 7

1. Why is Heidi compared to "a wild bird in a cage"?

   She is a girl of nature and has a difficult time adapting to a confined life in town.

2. Heidi is having a difficult start to her stay in Frankfurt. Miss Rottenmeier is very upset by Heidi's behavior, as shown in the first quote. Do you think Miss Rottenmeier is correct or incorrect in her assessment of Heidi's actions? Why?

   Have student(s) decide if they believe Heidi is truly "naughty" as Miss Rottenmeier says—Answers will vary.

3. From the second quote above, summarize what made Miss Rottenmeier anxious, annoyed, angry, and afraid.

   In short, Heidi's escapades for the day caused all these emotions. She was probably anxious when Heidi was missing, annoyed when Heidi ran out of the study room, upsetting the table's contents, angry with Heidi for leaving without permission, and afraid when the kittens were discovered.

Chapter 8

1. Read the quote above. Imagine you are Miss Rottenmeier and you don't know much about Heidi's life before she came to you. What about Heidi's quote above would seem strange to you?

   You wouldn't know who or what Snowflake is or why it would be crying. The sun doesn't talk to the mountains. The hawk croaking louder over Frankfurt because of the people in it just doesn't make much sense.

2. What is the relationship between Heidi and Sebastian? How has it changed since the beginning of Heidi's time in Frankfurt?

   Sebastian and Heidi have begun forging a friendship. He is starting to care for her and enjoy the fun she brings to the home. At the beginning, he was distant and somewhat scornful of Heidi.

3. Heidi's original plan was to go back to the mountains the day after she arrived in Frankfurt. In this chapter, she decides to stay. What are the reasons for her staying in Frankfurt?

   Miss Rottenmeier makes Heidi feel terrible for wanting to leave and will not allow her to do so. Clara also really wants her to stay, at least until her father returns. Heidi also comforts herself with the fact that she is able to save more rolls for Grannie the longer she stays.

Chapter 9

1. What is the relationship between Mr. Sesemann and Clara?

   They are a father and daughter who care very much about each other and enjoy spending time together.

2. In the second quote, what "matter" is Mr. Sesemann concerned about? Why is he concerned?

   Miss Rottenmeier thinks that Heidi may be insane. If she is, Clara could really be in danger.

3. How did Mr. Sesemann decide that Heidi should stay in Frankfurt?

   He tried talking to Miss Rottenmeier and Mr. Usher about Heidi, but at last he resorts to talking to Clara. Clara really enjoys having Heidi around and wants her to stay.

4. How was Heidi's errand to get water an example of her "funny little ways"?

   She ran down the street to get water from a fountain instead of getting water from inside the house. She isn't used to having water piped into the house.

Chapter 10

1. Describe Heidi's relationship with Grandmamma.

   Heidi loves and respects Grandmamma. She also learns about God and prayer from the old woman.

2. What results because of Heidi's realization in the third quote above?

   Heidi becomes heavyhearted, loses her appetite, and grows pale. She dreams about home and often cries when she wakes up.

3. How has being able to read made a difference in Heidi's life?

   Heidi has a whole new world opened up to her. She has great joy in reading.

4. Why do you think the story about the shepherd is Heidi's favorite?

   The story reminds her of her home and is about a boy going home, something Heidi wants desperately.

Chapter 11

1. Why does Heidi stop praying to God?

   Heidi thinks that God did not hear her prayer because He did not answer it right away. She figures He can't hear her anyway with all the other people praying.

2. Explain Grandmamma's answer to Heidi's disillusionment about unanswered prayer.

   Grandmamma tells Heidi that God doesn't always answer prayer the way we want or when we want. She says God knows more about what will be the best way. She also says Heidi should not turn her back on God because she will need him again.

3. Read the first quote above. Have you ever had an experience like this? What did you do to ease the loneliness?

   Answers will vary.

4. What are possible solutions to cure Heidi's homesickness in the second quote?

   Answers will vary.

Chapter 12

1. Mr. Sesemann has the doctor come and help him watch for the "ghost." Who or what does Mr. Sesemann think is responsible for the appearances?

   Mr. Sesemann thinks it might be some friends of the servants playing a trick on them. He also thinks it could be criminals trying to scare everyone into staying in their rooms.

2. How is the first vigil for the ghost different from the second?

   John and Sebastian believe in the ghost and are therefore more frightened. When John looks out and sees the "ghost," they lock themselves in the drawing room and don't come out until daylight. Mr. Sesemann and Dr. Classen don't believe in the ghost, so when they see it, they go out and confront it.

3. What is the scene depicted in the chapter's illustration?

   Dr. Classen and Mr. Sesemann find Heidi sleepwalking and opening the front door. She is confused and frightened when they question her.

Chapter 13

1. In the first quote above, why do you think Mr. Sesemann allows her to leave without any discussion?

   Answers will vary. Maybe he thinks it isn't worth wasting his time. He may not want to create a scene. He is a kind and generous man, so maybe he doesn't want to further embarrass Detie.

2. When Grandfather and Heidi first see each other again, he is unable to speak and has tears in his eyes for the first time in many years. When he does speak again he doesn't say how he feels about Heidi's return. Based on his actions, how do you think he feels about Heidi's return?

   It seems he is very glad to have her home. He is concerned about her health (gives her a glass of milk); he remakes her bed; he checks on her many times in the night.

3. Grandfather reads the letter from Mr. Sesemann, puts it in his pocket, and doesn't say anything about it. What do you think the letter says? Why would he not say anything?

   Answers will vary. We know it says something about the money because Grandfather tells Heidi she can buy a bed and clothes with it. Everything else is open to speculation.

Chapter 14

1. In the first quote above, what are some examples Heidi gives of how God knew what was best?

   If she hadn't stayed in Frankfurt, Heidi would not have been able to provide as many rolls for Grannie. She would not have been able to read, which brings great joy to Grannie.

2. The story of the prodigal son reappears in this chapter. What significance does the story have for Grandfather?

   The author portrays Grandfather as a type of prodigal son. He is now repentant before his Heavenly Father after many years of wandering, and even prays the same words the prodigal son spoke to his father.

3. Sometimes in stories the setting is a reflection of the characters' moods. Describe the setting of Sunday morning and tell how it might reflect Grandfather's and Heidi's moods.

   It was a beautiful sunny day, with bells pealing and birds singing. Both Grandfather and Heidi are dressed in their best outfits. They are full of joy (just like the day) as they head to church together.

4. In the second quote above, we see Grandfather at peace with God and man. What has he done to reach this place of peace?

   He has asked God's forgiveness, taken the step to go to church, asked the pastor's forgiveness, and agreed to live in Dorfli among the people during the winter.

Chapter 15

1. What is the context for the first quote? Do you think this is good encouragement, given the circumstances? Why or why not?

   Dr. Classen has just told Mr. Sesemann that he does not have much hope for Clara's full recovery. Answers will vary.

2. In the second quote above, how do you think the servants know before being told?

   Later in the chapter, Sebastian admits to overhearing some things from the dining room.

3. Clara packs many gifts for Heidi and those she loves. Discuss each gift and how it demonstrates Clara's thoughtfulness.

   The coat shows Clara listened carefully to Heidi's stories about going to Grannie's and recognized the need. The shawl is intended to keep Grannie warm and the cakes are to be a change from the rolls. She knows Peter would really enjoy a sausage and Grandfather would use the tobacco. All the gifts show that Clara listened to Heidi's stories in detail and thought about things to make their life more pleasant.

4. Clara's character shines through in this chapter. Give specific character traits you have observed and examples from the story.

   She is very generous (giving of the gifts); trusting (believes her father would only do what is best); patient (waiting on trip to Alps); selfless (if she can't go visit Heidi, she's glad Dr. Classen will) (Not an exhaustive list)

Chapter 16

1. What is the scene depicted in the chapter's illustration?

   The goats are crowding around Heidi and greeting her. Peter is on his way taking them up the mountain.

2. Heidi is really disappointed that Clara and Grandmamma cannot come. How does she respond to the disappointment? Have you ever experienced similar disappointment? How did you respond?

   Heidi is upset, but chooses to concentrate on the visitor she does have. She convinces herself that it would not be a long time before Clara really is able to come and begins to look forward to that. Answers will vary.

Chapter 17

1. What kinds of things do Grandfather and the doctor see on their long walks?

   They climb high up on the mountains, where the hawk nests. They explore many different kinds of plants and animals.

2. What makes Heidi volunteer to return to Frankfurt at the end of the chapter? Why is she encouraged to stay?

   The doctor says he wishes he could take Heidi back with him, and after he leaves, Heidi feels so miserable that she runs after him offering to go. The doctor is afraid she would become ill if she went back with him.

3. What clues help the reader predict that the doctor might someday return to Dorfli?

   The doctor "felt at home on the mountains." He had made friends with Grandfather, and he understood what a healing place it was. He didn't want to leave.

Chapter 18

1. How does Grandfather cause Peter to understand the true nature of his "desertion"?

   Grandfather asks Peter what he would do with goats that behaved the way he did. Peter realizes that he should be beaten like the goats.

2. Compare and contrast Peter and Heidi's views of school.

   Peter avoids school whenever possible and doesn't enjoy it. Heidi goes to school faithfully and tries to learn all that she can.

3. Heidi wants Grannie to be able to hear her hymns every day, but she can't go because of the snow. What are possible solutions to this problem?

   Answers will vary. Someone else might have to read to Grannie.

Chapter 19

1. What is Heidi referring to in the first quote? Do you think your attitude about an issue can affect how well you do it? Why?

   She is referring to Peter's reading ability. If you have a good attitude it will most likely increase your chances of succeeding. Answers will vary.

2. What is Peter's reaction to the rhymes Heidi uses?

   He takes them so personally that he believes they will come true! They sometimes aggravate him, but also serve to motivate him.

3. What is Uncle Alp's reaction to the lessons?

   He finds the exchange between Heidi and Peter to be very amusing.

4. What does the second quote tell you about Peter? Have you noticed this in him before?

   Peter can be lazy. He gives up far too easily—just over a difficult word. He is lackadaisical about school attendance and not willing to put forth much effort in learning to read. Other answers are possible.

Chapter 20

1. This chapter discloses some information about Uncle Alp's past. What do we learn about his former life? Does it fit with the story Detie told at the beginning?

   When Uncle Alp was a soldier, his captain was wounded in battle so that he could not move off the couch. Uncle Alp cared for him until he died. Detie confirms that he was in the army, but mentions a dishonorable discharge from it. This does not seem to be fact, but rather hearsay. It could be that he was discharged to care for his captain, but it is unclear.

2. What does Clara think of Heidi's home and the mountains?

   Clara loves everything about Heidi's home, so much so that she repeatedly uses a variation of "heavenly" to describe it.

3. What is being referred to in the second quote? Why does the speaker appreciate the offer?

   Uncle Alp offers to let Clara stay up on the mountains with them for several weeks. Grandmamma thinks the mountains would do Clara a lot of good and really wants her to stay, but does not want to impose upon Grandfather by asking him to care for her.

4. What is foresight? How does it avert misfortune? Do you have any examples from your experience where foresight has averted misfortune?

   Foresight is the act of looking forward. If you look forward and try to anticipate what may come, you can sometimes avoid the bad things through adequate preparation. In the story, Mrs. Sesemann prepares for the possibility of storms on the mountain by bringing extra blankets. Examples will vary.

Chapter 21

1. What is the context of the first quote? Why does the person look as though they "wanted to eat somebody"?

   Grandfather is giving instructions to Peter about Daisy. In the middle of his instructions, he breaks off to ask Peter this question. Peter is angry with Clara for taking Heidi away from him and so he scowls at her and ignores her whenever he is near.

2. What does the third quote tell us about Grandfather? Tell some examples of things he does to make Clara better?

   Grandfather is caring and thoughtful. He climbs high on the mountain to get herbs to make Daisy's milk better for Clara. He encourages Clara to spend time outdoors. Answers will vary.

Chapter 22

1. What are the consequences the person in the first quote experiences?

   Peter is miserable. He becomes very fearful and paranoid that he will be found out. He is so distraught that he cannot even eat his supper!

2. According to the second quote, why does Clara desire to be well? What does this tell you about her?

   Clara desires wellness so that she can serve others instead of always being the one who is served. It shows an unselfishness on her part. She doesn't want to be well just so she can play and do as she likes; she has nobler ambitions.

3. What is meant by the third quote?

   Clara has put forth the effort and has achieved something. The converse of that would be, "No pain, no gain." You cannot win anything without first giving effort.

4. Uncle Alp finds several things about the wheelchair's destruction to be unusual. Tell what observations he makes. Do you think he knows Peter destroyed it? Why?

   He notices that the wheelchair would have had to turn a corner to make it around the shed. He also finds it odd that Peter didn't see the ruins of the wheelchair on his way up the mountain. Answers will vary. (I think he does!)

Chapter 23

1. How does Mrs. Sesemann respond to Peter's confession of pushing the wheelchair over the mountain? Do you agree or disagree? Why?

   Mrs. Sesemann doesn't believe Peter would do such a thing at first. When she realizes he is responsible, she treats him with much kindness. She understands that Peter has felt very jealous of the time Heidi has given to Clara. She instructs him to remember how he felt this time when he is tempted to choose the wrong thing in the future. She then decides he needs no more punishment and instead gives him a gift to remember them by. Answers will vary.

2. This chapter holds the resolution to many different problems/conflicts that appear throughout the book. Try to list as many resolutions found in this chapter as possible. Discuss their significance.

   - Clara can walk and gets to show her grandmother and father.
   - Peter is forgiven and given a penny a week for life.
   - Heidi will be well taken care of after Grandfather passes on.
   - Grannie realizes Heidi will be staying on the mountains.
   - Grannie receives a bed to help her sleep better.
   - Mr. Sesemann is truly happy now that his daughter is well.
   - Dr. Classen retires and moves to the mountains.
   - Dr. Classen has Heidi to look after him when he is old, which brings him much joy.

   Answers will vary.

Quizzes & Final Test

Heidi Quiz 1

Chapters 1-5

Name ______________________________

Date ______________________________

Vocabulary Matching: Write the letter of the vocabulary word on the line. (10 points)

1. ______	exasperation	a.	separated
2. ______	morose	b.	poor
3. ______	extent	c.	offended; insulted
4. ______	detached	d.	to disagree with
5. ______	meagre	e.	great annoyance
6. ______	strenuous	f.	scope, limit, size
7. ______	impudence	g.	tough; active
8. ______	indignant	h.	boldness; disrespect
9. ______	wretchedly	i.	miserably
10. ______	contradict	j.	gloomy

Vocabulary Usage: Fill in the blank with the appropriate vocabulary word. (10 points)

amiability	**detached**	**obstinate**	**scudding**	**bellows**
indignant	**plunged**	**tremulously**		

1. Heidi is full of ______________________ towards her friend Peter, except when he is going to hurt the goats.
2. The goats became very hot from running about on the mountain. They ______________________ into the cool lake for a refreshing swim.
3. When Grandfather saw the fire dying, he used the ______________ to revive it.
4. "Finch is about to fall into the ravine!" Heidi cried ______________________.
5. The boy was being ______________________; he did not want to go and nothing could change his mind.

Identification: Circle the best answer(s) for each question. (10 points)

1. Heidi's parents: (circle two answers)
   a. Detie
   b. Adelheid
   c. Bridget
   d. Tobias
   e. Peter

2. Heidi's aunt who has taken care of her:

   a. Adelheid
   b. Ursula
   c. Barbie
   d. Detie

3. Who are the other two members of Peter's family?

   a. Tobias
   b. Bridget
   c. Barbie
   d. Grandfather
   e. Grannie

4. A narrow, steep-sided valley is a:

   a. summit
   b. hillock
   c. ravine
   d. loft

5. *"She can look after herself … She's got all her wits about her."* Who is this quote about?

   a. Detie
   b. Bridget
   c. Grannie
   d. Heidi

Comprehension Questions: Answer each question or fill in the blanks. (10 points)

1. Detie acquired Heidi because ______________________________.
2. The townspeople are ______________ to see Heidi going to stay with Uncle Alp.
3. Grandfather's goats are ______________________________.
4. Heidi helps save Finch by ______________________________.
5. Heidi is very upset during her visit to Grannie when she discovers ______________
   ______________________________.

Composition: Give two arguments Detie uses to convince Heidi to go with her to Frankfurt. (10 points)

____

____

____

____

____

____

Rubric and Points Possible:
Answer __/ 4 pts.; Capitalization __/ 2 pts.; Punctuation __/ 2 pts.; Complete Sentence __/ 2 pts.

Heidi Quiz 2

Chapters 6-9

Name ______________________________

Date ______________________________

Vocabulary Matching: Write the letter of the vocabulary word on the line. (10 points)

1. _______ crestfallen
2. _______ pompously
3. _______ encountered
4. _______ pert
5. _______ sojourn
6. _______ impertinent
7. _______ consoling
8. _______ summoned
9. _______ relish
10. _______ disdainful

a. bold; spirited
b. rude
c. comforting
d. diappointed
e. proudly; importantly
f. to call someone to appear
g. scornful
h. visit; temporary stay
i. to enjoy
j. to come upon or meet with

Vocabulary Usage: Fill in the blank with the appropriate vocabulary word. (10 points)

halfwitted	bear me out	peremptory	havoc	mimicking	waylaid

1. The parrot's owner was very surprised when the parrot began ____________________ everything he said.
2. The students were ______________________ by the teacher because they were running through the halls.
3. Miss Rottenmeier wondered if Heidi was ____________________ because of her unusual behavior.
4. A bird flew in one of the restaurant's open windows, causing great ________________________ among the customers and servers.
5. The child was instructed not to use a ___________________________ tone when speaking with adults.

Identification: Circle the best answer(s) for each question. (10 points)

1. Housekeeper in charge of the servants and caring for Clara:

   a. Detie
   b. Tinette
   c. Miss Rottenmeier

2. Wealthy owner of home in Frankfurt; Clara's father:
    a. Mr. Sesemann
    b. Mr. Usher
    c. John
    d. Sebastian
3. Clara's tutor:
    a. Mr. Sesemann
    b. Mr. Usher
    c. John
    d. Sebastian
4. *"You told me you wanted an unusual sort of child ..."* Who says this?
    a. Miss Rottenmeier
    b. Mr. Sesemann
    c. Mr. Usher
    d. Detie
5. *"I think even Swiss children must put their feet on the ground ..."* Who says this?
    a. Miss Rottenmeier
    b. Mr. Sesemann
    c. Mr. Usher
    d. Detie

Comprehension Questions: Answer each question or fill in the blanks. (10 points)

1. Miss Rottenmeier is ______________________ with Heidi when she first meets her.
2. Miss Rottenmeier tries to get ________________ to help in her plot to send Heidi home.
3. Heidi tries to find a place in the city where ____________________________________
    ____.
4. Mr. Usher is worried about Heidi because ____________________________________
    ____.
5. On Heidi's trip to fetch water, she meets and talks with ____________________________.

Composition: What is Miss Rottenmeier's ideal image of a companion for Clara? Do you think Heidi makes a good companion for Clara? Why or why not? (10 points)

____

____

____

____

____

____

Rubric and Points Possible:
Answer __/ 4 pts.; Capitalization __/ 2 pts.; Punctuation __/ 2 pts.; Complete Sentence __/ 2 pts.

Heidi Quiz 3

Chapters 10-13

Name ______________________________

Date ______________________________

Vocabulary Matching: Write the letter of the vocabulary word on the line. (10 points)

1. _______	vexing	a.	suddenly
2. _______	inclination	b.	lonely; sad
3. _______	penitently	c.	intention
4. _______	forlorn	d.	desperately begging
5. _______	peaky	e.	insincerely
6. _______	fortify	f.	irritating
7. _______	precipitately	g.	feeling sorry for sin or wrongdoing
8. _______	robust	h.	sickly; pale
9. _______	glibly	i.	to strengthen
10. _______	imploring	j.	strong; healthy

Vocabulary Usage: Fill in the blank with the appropriate vocabulary word. (10 points)

dainty	**deprived**	**disheveled**	**fervently**	**grimaces**
rouse	**vividly**			

1. The politician spoke ______________________ about sending food to people in desperate need of help.
2. The student's mother found he was difficult to ______________________ on the first day of school; he had been used to sleeping in during the summer.
3. The dog's fur was very __________________________ after being shook dry.
4. Grandma's tea set is ___________________; you have to be careful when using it.
5. The girl was grounded and her mother had _________________________her of watching television.

Identification: Circle the best answer(s) for each question. (10 points)

1. *"… you've never learnt to read because you believed what Peter told you."* Who says this?
   a. Detie
   b. Clara
   c. Miss Rottenmeier
   d. Grandmamma

2. *"The front door was wide open and there was a white figure …"* Who says this?

   a. Mr. Sesemann
   b. Mr. Usher
   c. John
   d. Sebastian

3. *"Fright might even … bring on an attack of St. Vitus' dance."* Who writes this?

   a. Miss Rottenmeier
   b. Mr. Usher
   c. Mr. Sesemann
   d. Dr. Classen

4. *"I must ask you not to cast reflections on my entirely respectable forbears!"* To whom is this spoken?

   a. Mr. Sesemann
   b. Miss Rottenmeier
   c. Mr. Usher
   d. Detie

5. *"This is not an illness that can be cured with pills and powders."* Who says this?

   a. Miss Rottenmeier
   b. Mr. Sesemann
   c. Mr. Usher
   d. Dr. Classen

Comprehension Questions: Answer each question or fill in the blanks. (10 points)

1. Heidi learns to read because ____________________ convinces her she will be able.
2. When Heidi is crying, Miss Rottenmeier threatens to ____________________________________.
3. After seeing the "ghost," the next thing John does is ____________________________________
   ____.
4. Miss Rottenmeier tells Clara about the ghost, so that ____________________________________
   ____.
5. The townspeople thinks Heidi has returned because she has been treated ____________________.

Composition: Grandmamma notices that Heidi is sad. Why is she sad? Why does she keep the reason a secret? To whom does Heidi tell her feelings? (10 points)

____

____

____

____

____

____

Rubric and Points Possible:
Answer __/ 4 pts.; Capitalization __/ 2 pts.; Punctuation __/ 2 pts.; Complete Sentence __/ 2 pts.

Heidi Quiz 4

Chapters 14-18

Name ______________________________

Date ______________________________

Vocabulary Matching: Write the letter of the vocabulary word on the line. (10 points)

1. _______ careworn
2. _______ forsakes
3. _______ resigned
4. _______ wryly
5. _______ faculty
6. _______ boisterous
7. _______ aloof
8. _______ fleeting
9. _______ scowled
10. _______ cryptic

a. noisy
b. mysterious
c. worried
d. ability; skill
e. frowned and glared
f. at a distance
g. leaving one's duty without permission
h. accepting or unresisting
i. temporary; passing quickly
j. amused by something ironic or contrary

Vocabulary Usage: Fill in the blank with the appropriate vocabulary word. (10 points)

agile	**desertion**	**intrusion**	**obstreperous**	**prospect**
spick and span	**tussle**			

1. The older sister put a "KEEP OUT" sign on her door to prevent the ______________________ of her younger brother.
2. The children were excited by the ______________ of their grandparents coming.
3. The kitchen floor was ______________________ after being swept and mopped.
4. We keep the cat and dog in separate rooms to prevent a ________________ between them.
5. The ballet class was very ______________; they were able to move with ease and beauty.

Identification: Circle the best answer(s) for each question. (10 points)

1. *"God knew what was best … see how perfectly He arranged everything."* Who says this?
   a. Heidi
   b. Clara
   c. Grandfather
   d. the pastor in Dorfli
2. *"It's good to feel at peace with God and man."* Who says this?
   a. Mr. Sesemann
   b. Dr. Classen
   c. Grandfather
   d. the pastor in Dorfli

3. *"Oh, it will soon be spring. Time goes quickly up here."* To whom is this spoken?

   a. Heidi
   b. Clara
   c. Grandfather
   d. Dr. Classen

4. *"This is certainly the place for Clara to come to. She would soon become a different person …"* Who says this?

   a. Mr. Sesemann
   b. Grandfather
   c. Dr. Classen
   d. Heidi

5. *"Life really seems worth living again!"* Who says this?

   a. Grandfather
   b. Grannie
   c. Heidi
   d. Dr. Classen

Comprehension Questions: Answer each question or fill in the blanks. (10 points)

1. After Grandfather leaves the parsonage, the townspeople are eager to ______________________ ____.
2. Clara is unable to visit Heidi because ______________________________.
3. Heidi tries to comfort ______________________ when she sees his sadness.
4. Peter is very ______________________ about all the time Heidi and the doctor spend together.
5. Grannie is secretly worried that ______________________________ ____.

Composition: What words of wisdom does Heidi give the doctor? What is the role reversal of the conversation? (10 points)

____

____

____

____

____

____

Rubric and Points Possible:
Answer __/ 4 pts.; Capitalization __/ 2 pts.; Punctuation __/ 2 pts.; Complete Sentence __/ 2 pts.

Heidi Quiz 5

Chapters 19-23

Name ______________________

Date ______________________

Vocabulary Matching: Write the letter of the vocabulary word on the line. (10 points)

1. _______ bewildered
2. _______ cocky
3. _______ trifle
4. _______ avert
5. _______ disperse
6. _______ extricate
7. _______ ecstatically
8. _______ profusion
9. _______ improvise
10. _______ conviction

a. to ward off or prevent
b. firm belief
c. with joyful excitement
d. being too proud of oneself
e. a great amount
f. to untangle
g. to make or do something at the spur of the moment
h. confused
i. to spread out or scatter
j. a little bit or small amount

Vocabulary Usage: Fill in the blank with the appropriate vocabulary word. (10 points)

agonized	**brandishing**	**exertions**	**exquisite**	**expedition**
squarely	**passionately**	**resentment**		

1. The hikers set out on an ______________________ through the forest.
2. When the hikers finished their hike they were worn out from their ______________________.
3. The child felt ______________________ because she was not invited to her friend's birthday party.
4. The painting was ______________________; it showed the artist had used great care and detail in creating it.
5. John had an ______________________ expression on his face as he told his mother how he had broken her favorite vase.

Identification: Circle the best answer(s) for each question. (10 points)

1. *"As long as I can remember I've only eaten because I had to … here, I can hardly wait for your grandfather to bring my milk."* Who says this?
   a. Heidi
   b. Clara
   c. Grandmamma
   d. Peter

2. *"The real badness of what he had done had not yet occurred to him …"* This quote refers to whom?

   a. Mr. Sesemann
   b. Dr. Classen
   c. Grandfather
   d. Peter

3. *"Foresight is a virtue and averts many a misfortune."* Who says this?

   a. Heidi
   b. Clara
   c. Grandfather
   d. Grandmamma

4. *"Something attempted, something won."* To whom is this spoken?

   a. Mr. Sesemann
   b. Grandfather
   c. Clara
   d. Heidi

5. *"Heidi's going to stay here with you … we shall come to her …"* Who says this?

   a. Grandfather
   b. Grannie
   c. Grandmamma
   d. Mr. Sesemann

Comprehension Questions: Answer each question or fill in the blanks. (10 points)

1. Heidi convinces Peter to let her teach him how to ________________ .
2. Heidi is ________________ and Peter is ________________ about the visitors coming from Frankfurt.
3. Uncle Alp helps Clara learn to ________________________________ by having her practice a little longer each day.
4. Some people thought that ________________ blew the wheelchair down the mountain.
5. When Peter runs into Mr. Sesemann, Peter thinks he is ________________________.

Composition: After reading the whole story, what can be said about Heidi's and Clara's friendship? (10 points)

____

____

____

____

____

____

Rubric and Points Possible:
Answer __/ 4 pts.; Capitalization __/ 2 pts.; Punctuation __/ 2 pts.; Complete Sentence __/ 2 pts.

Heidi Final Test

Chapters 19-23

Name ______________________________

Date ______________________________

Vocabulary Usage: Fill in the blank with the appropriate vocabulary word. (20 points)

amiability	**agonized**	**dainty**	**exquisite**	**halfwitted**
havoc	**obstinate**	**prospect**	**rouse**	**tussle**

1. The boy was being ______________________; he did not want to change his clothes for pictures and nothing could change his mind.
2. The two brothers were sent to their rooms as punishment after they had a ______________.
3. The sculpture was ______________________; it showed the artist had used great care and detail in creating it.
4. Susan had an ______________________ expression on her face as she told her mother how she had fallen and injured herself.
5. Mother's fine china is very ______________; you have to be careful when using it.
6. The children were excited by the ______________ of their grandparents coming.
7. We had to ______________ Dad for dinner—he had fallen asleep on the couch.
8. Grandmamma wondered if Peter was ______________________ when he talked about destroying her flowers.
9. The baseball was hit into our section of seats, causing great ______________ among everyone around us.
10. Clara almost always speaks with ____________________ to Heidi, which is part of the reason they get along so well.

Identification: Circle the best answer(s) for each question. (30 points)

1. Heidi's aunt who has taken care of her:
   a. Adelheid
   b. Ursula
   c. Barbie
   d. Detie
2. Who are the other two members of Peter's family?
   a. Tobias
   b. Bridget
   c. Barbie
   d. Grannie
3. Housekeeper in charge of the servants and caring for Clara:
   a. Detie
   b. Tinette
   c. Miss Rottenmeier

4. *"You told me you wanted an unusual sort of child …"* Who says this?
    a. Miss Rottenmeier
    b. Mr. Sesemann
    c. Mr. Usher
    d. Detie
5. *"This is not an illness that can be cured with pills and powders."* Who says this?
    a. Miss Rottenmeier
    b. Mr. Sesemann
    c. Mr. Usher
    d. Dr. Classen
6. *"… you've never learnt to read because you believed what Peter told you."* Who says this?
    a. Detie
    b. Clara
    c. Miss Rottenmeier
    d. Grandmamma
7. *"It's good to feel at peace with God and man."* Who says this?
    a. Mr. Sesemann
    b. Dr. Classen
    c. Grandfather
    d. the pastor in Dorfli
8. *"God knew what was best … see how perfectly He arranged everything."* Who says this?
    a. Heidi
    b. Clara
    c. Grandfather
    d. the pastor in Dorfli
9. *"The real badness of what he had done had not yet occurred to him …"* This quote refers to whom?
    a. Mr. Sesemann
    b. Dr. Classen
    c. Grandfather
    d. Peter
10. *"Something attempted, something won."* To whom is this spoken?
    a. Mr. Sesemann
    b. Grandfather
    c. Clara
    d. Heidi

True or False: For each statement write "T" if true and "F" if false. (40 points)

1. _____ The townspeople are glad to see Heidi going to stay with Uncle Alp because they respect him.
2. _____ Heidi is very upset when she discovers Grannie is blind and thinks Grandfather will be able to heal her.
3. _____ Miss Rottenmeier is understanding of Heidi's homesickness and tries to comfort her.
4. _____ Miss Rottenmeier thinks Heidi is the ideal companion for Clara.
5. _____ Heidi learns to read because Mr. Usher begs her to try harder.

6. _____ After seeing the "ghost," John walks around the house trying to find it.
7. _____ After Grandfather leaves the parsonage, the townspeople are eager to talk to him and invite him into their homes.
8. _____ Grannie is worried that someone will take Heidi back to Frankfurt.
9. _____ Heidi and Peter are overjoyed about the visitors coming from Frankfurt.
10. _____ Uncle Alp helps Clara learn to stand on her own by having her stand a little longer each day.

Composition: Grandmamma notices that Heidi is sad. Why is she sad? Why does she keep the reason a secret? To whom does Heidi tell her feelings? (5 points)

____

____

____

____

____

____

Rubric and Points Possible:
Answer __/ 3 pts.; Capitalization & Punctuation __/ 2 pts.

Composition: After reading the whole story, what can be said about Heidi's and Clara's friendship? (5 points)

____

____

____

____

____

____

Rubric and Points Possible:
Answer __/ 3 pts.; Capitalization & Punctuation __/ 2 pts.

Heidi Quiz 1 Answer Key

Chapters 1-5

Name ______________________________

Date ______________________________

Vocabulary Matching: Write the letter of the vocabulary word on the line. (10 points)

1. E exasperation
2. J morose
3. F extent
4. A detached
5. B meagre
6. G strenuous
7. H impudence
8. C indignant
9. I wretchedly
10. D contradict

a. separated
b. poor
c. offended; insulted
d. to disagree with
e. great annoyance
f. scope, limit, size
g. tough; active
h. boldness; disrespect
i. miserably
j. gloomy

Vocabulary Usage: Fill in the blank with the appropriate vocabulary word. (10 points)

amiability	**detached**	**obstinate**	**scudding**	**bellows**
indignant	**plunged**	**tremulously**		

1. Heidi is full of amiability towards her friend Peter, except when he is going to hurt the goats.
2. The goats became very hot from running about on the mountain. They plunged into the cool lake for a refreshing swim.
3. When Grandfather saw the fire dying, he used the bellows to revive it.
4. "Finch is about to fall into the ravine!" Heidi cried tremulously.
5. The boy was being obstinate; he did not want to go and nothing could change his mind.

Identification: Circle the best answer(s) for each question. (10 points)

1. Heidi's parents: (circle two answers)
   a. Detie
   (b.) Adelheid
   c. Bridget
   (d.) Tobias
   e. Peter

2. Heidi's aunt who has taken care of her:
   a. Adelheid
   b. Ursula
   c. Barbie
   (d.) Detie
3. Who are the other two members of Peter's family?
   a. Tobias
   (b.) Bridget
   c. Barbie
   d. Grandfather
   (e.) Grannie
4. A narrow, steep-sided valley is a:
   a. summit
   b. hillock
   (c.) ravine
   d. loft
5. *"She can look after herself … She's got all her wits about her."* Who is this quote about?
   a. Detie
   b. Bridget
   c. Grannie
   (d.) Heidi

Comprehension Questions: Answer each question or fill in the blanks. (10 points)

1. Detie acquired Heidi because her parents and grandmother had died.
2. The townspeople are upset; concerned to see Heidi going to stay with Uncle Alp.
3. Grandfather's goats are Daisy and Dusky.
4. Heidi helps save Finch by luring him away from the ravine by offering him grass.
5. Heidi is very upset during her visit to Grannie when she discovers that Grannie is blind and that she fears the house falling in on them.

Composition: Give two arguments Detie uses to convince Heidi to go with her to Frankfurt. (10 points)

Possible answers: 1) Detie tells Heidi that Grandfather is very upset and he wants Heidi to go with her. 2) Detie says that Heidi can come back to the mountains any time she wants, if she is not happy in Frankfurt. 3) Detie promises that Heidi can bring back a present of white rolls for Grannie.

Rubric and Points Possible:
Answer __/ 4 pts.; Capitalization __/ 2 pts.; Punctuation __/ 2 pts.; Complete Sentence __/ 2 pts.

Heidi Quiz 2 Answer Key

Chapters 6-9

Name ______________________

Date ______________________

Vocabulary Matching: Write the letter of the vocabulary word on the line. (10 points)

1. D crestfallen
2. E pompously
3. J encountered
4. A pert
5. H sojourn
6. B impertinent
7. C consoling
8. F summoned
9. I relish
10. G disdainful

a. bold; spirited
b. rude
c. comforting
d. diappointed
e. proudly; importantly
f. to call someone to appear
g. scornful
h. visit; temporary stay
i. to enjoy
j. to come upon or meet with

Vocabulary Usage: Fill in the blank with the appropriate vocabulary word. (10 points)

halfwitted	bear me out	peremptory	havoc	mimicking	waylaid

1. The parrot's owner was very surprised when the parrot began mimicking everything he said.
2. The students were waylaid by the teacher because they were running through the halls.
3. Miss Rottenmeier wondered if Heidi was halfwitted because of her unusual behavior.
4. A bird flew in one of the restaurant's open windows, causing great havoc among the customers and servers.
5. The child was instructed not to use a peremptory tone when speaking with adults.

Identification: Circle the best answer(s) for each question. (10 points)

1. Housekeeper in charge of the servants and caring for Clara:
   a. Detie
   b. Tinette
   (c.) Miss Rottenmeier

2. Wealthy owner of home in Frankfurt; Clara's father:

   (a.) Mr. Sesemann
   b. Mr. Usher
   c. John
   d. Sebastian

3. Clara's tutor:

   a. Mr. Sesemann
   (b.) Mr. Usher
   c. John
   d. Sebastian

4. *"You told me you wanted an unusual sort of child …"* Who says this?

   a. Miss Rottenmeier
   b. Mr. Sesemann
   c. Mr. Usher
   (d.) Detie

5. *"I think even Swiss children must put their feet on the ground …"* Who says this?

   a. Miss Rottenmeier
   (b.) Mr. Sesemann
   c. Mr. Usher
   d. Detie

Comprehension Questions: Answer each question or fill in the blanks. (10 points)

1. Miss Rottenmeier is unimpressed/disappointed with Heidi when she first meets her.
2. Miss Rottenmeier tries to get Mr. Usher/tutor to help in her plot to send Heidi home.
3. Heidi tries to find a place in the city where she can see nature/the mountains.
4. Mr. Usher is worried about Heidi because she has not learned the alphabet/how to read.
5. On Heidi's trip to fetch water, she meets and talks with the doctor/Dr. Classen.

Composition: What is Miss Rottenmeier's ideal image of a companion for Clara? Do you think Heidi makes a good companion for Clara? Why or why not? (10 points)

Miss Rottenmeier would prefer someone Clara's own age who knows how to read and behave in polite society. Answers will vary.

Rubric and Points Possible:
Answer __/ 4 pts.; Capitalization __/ 2 pts.; Punctuation __/ 2 pts.; Complete Sentence __/ 2 pts.

Heidi Quiz 3 Answer Key

Chapters 10-13

Name ______________________

Date ______________________

Vocabulary Matching: Write the letter of the vocabulary word on the line. (10 points)

1. F vexing
2. C inclination
3. G penitently
4. B forlorn
5. H peaky
6. I fortify
7. A precipitately
8. J robust
9. E glibly
10. D imploring

a. suddenly
b. lonely; sad
c. intention
d. desperately begging
e. insincerely
f. irritating
g. feeling sorry for sin or wrongdoing
h. sickly; pale
i. to strengthen
j. strong; healthy

Vocabulary Usage: Fill in the blank with the appropriate vocabulary word. (10 points)

dainty	**deprived**	**disheveled**	**fervently**	**grimaces**
rouse	**vividly**			

1. The politician spoke fervently about sending food to people in desperate need of help.
2. The student's mother found he was difficult to rouse on the first day of school; he had been used to sleeping in during the summer.
3. The dog's fur was very disheveled after being shook dry.
4. Grandma's tea set is dainty; you have to be careful when using it.
5. The girl was grounded and her mother had deprived her of watching television.

Identification: Circle the best answer(s) for each question. (10 points)

1. *"… you've never learnt to read because you believed what Peter told you."* Who says this?
   a. Detie
   b. Clara
   c. Miss Rottenmeier
   (d.) Grandmamma

2. *"The front door was wide open and there was a white figure …"* Who says this?

   a. Mr. Sesemann
   b. Mr. Usher
   (c.) John
   d. Sebastian

3. *"Fright might even … bring on an attack of St. Vitus' dance."* Who writes this?

   (a.) Miss Rottenmeier
   b. Mr. Usher
   c. Mr. Sesemann
   d. Dr. Classen

4. *"I must ask you not to cast reflections on my entirely respectable forbears!"* To whom is this spoken?

   a. Mr. Sesemann
   (b.) Miss Rottenmeier
   c. Mr. Usher
   d. Detie

5. *"This is not an illness that can be cured with pills and powders."* Who says this?

   a. Miss Rottenmeier
   b. Mr. Sesemann
   c. Mr. Usher
   (d.) Dr. Classen

Comprehension Questions: Answer each question or fill in the blanks. (10 points)

1. Heidi learns to read because Grandmamma convinces her she will be able.
2. When Heidi is crying, Miss Rottenmeier threatens to take away her book.
3. After seeing the "ghost," the next thing John does is run back into the room, shut the door, and stay in the room until daylight.
4. Miss Rottenmeier tells Clara about the ghost, so that Mr. Sesemann will return home to take care of it.
5. The townspeople thinks Heidi has returned because she has been treated badly.

Composition: Grandmamma notices that Heidi is sad. Why is she sad? Why does she keep the reason a secret? To whom does Heidi tell her feelings? (10 points)

Heidi is sad because she realizes she cannot go home any time she wants to. She doesn't want to tell anyone about it because she doesn't want the Sesemanns to think she is ungrateful. Grandmamma encourages Heidi to tell God about her feelings.

Rubric and Points Possible:
Answer __/ 4 pts.; Capitalization __/ 2 pts.; Punctuation __/ 2 pts.; Complete Sentence __/ 2 pts.

Heidi Quiz 4 Answer Key

Chapters 14-18

Name ______________________

Date ______________________

Vocabulary Matching: Write the letter of the vocabulary word on the line. (10 points)

1. C careworn
2. G forsakes
3. H resigned
4. J wryly
5. D faculty
6. A boisterous
7. F aloof
8. I fleeting
9. E scowled
10. B cryptic

a. noisy
b. mysterious
c. worried
d. ability; skill
e. frowned and glared
f. at a distance
g. leaving one's duty without permission
h. accepting or unresisting
i. temporary; passing quickly
j. amused by something ironic or contrary

Vocabulary Usage: Fill in the blank with the appropriate vocabulary word. (10 points)

agile	desertion	intrusion	obstreperous	prospect
spick and span	tussle			

1. The older sister put a "KEEP OUT" sign on her door to prevent the intrusion of her younger brother.
2. The children were excited by the prospect of their grandparents coming.
3. The kitchen floor was spick and span after being swept and mopped.
4. We keep the cat and dog in separate rooms to prevent a tussle between them.
5. The ballet class was very agile; they were able to move with ease and beauty.

Identification: Circle the best answer(s) for each question. (10 points)

1. *"God knew what was best … see how perfectly He arranged everything."* Who says this?
   - (a.) Heidi
   - b. Clara
   - c. Grandfather
   - d. the pastor in Dorfli
2. *"It's good to feel at peace with God and man."* Who says this?
   - a. Mr. Sesemann
   - b. Dr. Classen
   - (c.) Grandfather
   - d. the pastor in Dorfli

3. *"Oh, it will soon be spring. Time goes quickly up here."* To whom is this spoken?

   a. Heidi
   b. Clara
   c. Grandfather
   (d.) Dr. Classen

4. *"This is certainly the place for Clara to come to. She would soon become a different person …"* Who says this?

   a. Mr. Sesemann
   b. Grandfather
   (c.) Dr. Classen
   d. Heidi

5. *"Life really seems worth living again!"* Who says this?

   a. Grandfather
   b. Grannie
   c. Heidi
   (d.) Dr. Classen

Comprehension Questions: Answer each question or fill in the blanks. (10 points)

1. After Grandfather leaves the parsonage, the townspeople are eager to shake hands and invite him into their homes/greet him and welcome him back.
2. Clara is unable to visit Heidi because she is not well/she is too ill to travel.
3. Heidi tries to comfort the doctor/Dr. Classen when she sees his sadness.
4. Peter is very jealous/upset about all the time Heidi and the doctor spend together.
5. Grannie is secretly worried that someone will take Heidi back to Frankfurt.

Composition: What words of wisdom does Heidi give the doctor? What is the role reversal of the conversation? (10 points)

She tells him to trust God during difficult times. This is a role reversal because Heidi is taking the "adult" role and comforting the doctor.

Rubric and Points Possible:
Answer __/ 4 pts.; Capitalization __/ 2 pts.; Punctuation __/ 2 pts.; Complete Sentence __/ 2 pts.

Heidi Quiz 5 Answer Key

Chapters 19-23

Name ______________________

Date ______________________

Vocabulary Matching: Write the letter of the vocabulary word on the line. (10 points)

1. H bewildered
2. D cocky
3. J trifle
4. A avert
5. I disperse
6. F extricate
7. C ecstatically
8. E profusion
9. G improvise
10. B conviction

a. to ward off or prevent
b. firm belief
c. with joyful excitement
d. being too proud of oneself
e. a great amount
f. to untangle
g. to make or do something at the spur of the moment
h. confused
i. to spread out or scatter
j. a little bit or small amount

Vocabulary Usage: Fill in the blank with the appropriate vocabulary word. (10 points)

agonized	**brandishing**	**exertions**	**exquisite**	**expedition**
squarely	**passionately**	**resentment**		

1. The hikers set out on an expedition through the forest.
2. When the hikers finished their hike they were worn out from their exertions.
3. The child felt resentment because she was not invited to her friend's birthday party.
4. The painting was exquisite; it showed the artist had used great care and detail in creating it.
5. John had an agonized expression on his face as he told his mother how he had broken her favorite vase.

Identification: Circle the best answer(s) for each question. (10 points)

1. *"As long as I can remember I've only eaten because I had to … here, I can hardly wait for your grandfather to bring my milk."* Who says this?

   a. Heidi
   (b.) Clara
   c. Grandmamma
   d. Peter

2. *"The real badness of what he had done had not yet occurred to him …"* This quote refers to whom?
   a. Mr. Sesemann
   b. Dr. Classen
   c. Grandfather
   (d.) Peter
3. *"Foresight is a virtue and averts many a misfortune."* Who says this?
   a. Heidi
   b. Clara
   c. Grandfather
   (d.) Grandmamma
4. *"Something attempted, something won."* To whom is this spoken?
   a. Mr. Sesemann
   b. Grandfather
   (c.) Clara
   d. Heidi
5. *"Heidi's going to stay here with you … we shall come to her …"* Who says this?
   a. Grandfather
   b. Grannie
   (c.) Grandmamma
   d. Mr. Sesemann

Comprehension Questions: Answer each question or fill in the blanks. (10 points)

1. Heidi convinces Peter to let her teach him how to ___read___.
2. Heidi is ___overjoyed/excited___ and Peter is ___angry/jealous___ about the visitors coming from Frankfurt.
3. Uncle Alp helps Clara learn to ___stand on her own/walk___ by having her practice a little longer each day.
4. Some people thought that ___the wind___ blew the wheelchair down the mountain.
5. When Peter runs into Mr. Sesemann, Peter thinks he is ___a policeman coming for him___.

Composition: After reading the whole story, what can be said about Heidi's and Clara's friendship? (10 points)

Their friendship was very strong, and would probably last a lifetime. They had learned a great deal from one another.

Rubric and Points Possible:
Answer __/ 4 pts.; Capitalization __/ 2 pts.; Punctuation __/ 2 pts.; Complete Sentence __/ 2 pts.

Heidi Final Test Answer Key

Chapters 19-23

Name ______________________

Date ______________________

Vocabulary Usage: Fill in the blank with the appropriate vocabulary word. (20 points)

amiability	agonized	dainty	exquisite	halfwitted
havoc	obstinate	prospect	rouse	tussle

1. The boy was being ___obstinate___; he did not want to change his clothes for pictures and nothing could change his mind.
2. The two brothers were sent to their rooms as punishment after they had a ___tussle___.
3. The sculpture was ___exquisite___; it showed the artist had used great care and detail in creating it.
4. Susan had an ___agonized___ expression on her face as she told her mother how she had fallen and injured herself.
5. Mother's fine china is very ___dainty___; you have to be careful when using it.
6. The children were excited by the ___prospect___ of their grandparents coming.
7. We had to ___rouse___ Dad for dinner—he had fallen asleep on the couch.
8. Grandmamma wondered if Peter was ___halfwitted___ when he talked about destroying her flowers.
9. The baseball was hit into our section of seats, causing great ___havoc___ among everyone around us.
10. Clara almost always speaks with ___amiability___ to Heidi, which is part of the reason they get along so well.

Identification: Circle the best answer(s) for each question. (30 points)

1. Heidi's aunt who has taken care of her:
   - a. Adelheid
   - b. Ursula
   - c. Barbie
   - (d.) Detie
2. Who are the other two members of Peter's family?
   - a. Tobias
   - (b.) Bridget
   - c. Barbie
   - (d.) Grannie
3. Housekeeper in charge of the servants and caring for Clara:
   - a. Detie
   - b. Tinette
   - (c.) Miss Rottenmeier

4. *"You told me you wanted an unusual sort of child ..."* Who says this?
   a. Miss Rottenmeier
   b. Mr. Sesemann
   c. Mr. Usher
   (d.) Detie
5. *"This is not an illness that can be cured with pills and powders."* Who says this?
   a. Miss Rottenmeier
   b. Mr. Sesemann
   c. Mr. Usher
   (d.) Dr. Classen
6. *"... you've never learnt to read because you believed what Peter told you."* Who says this?
   a. Detie
   b. Clara
   c. Miss Rottenmeier
   (d.) Grandmamma
7. *"It's good to feel at peace with God and man."* Who says this?
   a. Mr. Sesemann
   b. Dr. Classen
   (c.) Grandfather
   d. the pastor in Dorfli
8. *"God knew what was best ... see how perfectly He arranged everything."* Who says this?
   (a.) Heidi
   b. Clara
   c. Grandfather
   d. the pastor in Dorfli
9. *"The real badness of what he had done had not yet occurred to him ..."* This quote refers to whom?
   a. Mr. Sesemann
   b. Dr. Classen
   c. Grandfather
   (d.) Peter
10. *"Something attempted, something won."* To whom is this spoken?
   a. Mr. Sesemann
   b. Grandfather
   (c.) Clara
   d. Heidi

True or False: For each statement write "T" if true and "F" if false. (40 points)

1. __F__ The townspeople are glad to see Heidi going to stay with Uncle Alp because they respect him.
2. __T__ Heidi is very upset when she discovers Grannie is blind and thinks Grandfather will be able to heal her.
3. __F__ Miss Rottenmeier is understanding of Heidi's homesickness and tries to comfort her.
4. __F__ Miss Rottenmeier thinks Heidi is the ideal companion for Clara.
5. __F__ Heidi learns to read because Mr. Usher begs her to try harder.

6. __F__ After seeing the “ghost,” John walks around the house trying to find it.
7. __T__ After Grandfather leaves the parsonage, the townspeople are eager to talk to him and invite him into their homes.
8. __T__ Grannie is worried that someone will take Heidi back to Frankfurt.
9. __F__ Heidi and Peter are overjoyed about the visitors coming from Frankfurt.
10. __T__ Uncle Alp helps Clara learn to stand on her own by having her stand a little longer each day.

Composition: Grandmamma notices that Heidi is sad. Why is she sad? Why does she keep the reason a secret? To whom does Heidi tell her feelings? (5 points)

Heidi is sad because she realizes she cannot go home any time she wants to. She doesn’t want to tell anyone about it because she doesn’t want the Sesemanns to think she is ungrateful. Grandmamma encourages Heidi to tell God about her feelings.

Rubric and Points Possible:
Answer __/ 3 pts.; Capitalization & Punctuation __/ 2 pts.

Composition: After reading the whole story, what can be said about Heidi’s and Clara’s friendship? (5 points)

Their friendship was very strong, and would probably last a lifetime. They had learned a great deal from one another.

Rubric and Points Possible:
Answer __/ 3 pts.; Capitalization & Punctuation __/ 2 pts.